THE LIFE THAT JACK LIVED

Experiences of a Norfolk soldier and policeman

JACK TROUP

Larks Press

Published by the Larks Press
Ordnance Farmhouse
Guist Bottom, Dereham, Norfolk
NR20 5PF
01328 829207

September 1997

Printed by the Lanceni Press, Fakenham, Norfolk

British Library Cataloguing-in-Publication Data
A catalogue record for this book is available
at the British Library

The publishers wish to thank Brenda Gamlin of Old Hall,
East Bergholt for permission to use the photograph on p. 11 and
David Yaxley for the photograph on p. 27

ISBN 0 948400 56 0

*To my wife Valerie
without whose interest I would
never have completed this book*

Myself, aged 3½ years, and my sister Hilda
aged 18 months

Chapter 1. - Gateshead

—❊—

I, John James Richard Troup, was born on March 21st, 1918, at Gateshead, County Durham. My father was with the Durham Light Infantry in Germany and took part in the occupation of Cologne. When he came out of the army he went back to the mines at Seaham Harbour. I never saw him again.

With the disappearance of my father, my mother went to a college in London to learn to cook, leaving me and my sister in the charge of her mother, my gran, who was the sister of Joseph Mallaby Dent, the founder of the publishing firm of J. M. Dent.

My sister and I lived with my granny until the middle of 1928 when she became ill. My sister was then sent to an orphanage, whereabouts I don't know, but I was left with my gran and looked after her the best way I could until one day an ambulance came and took her away and I was put into the workhouse. I had no friends any more, the furniture all went, and what little toys and books I had all disappeared.

I think I was in the workhouse for about three months and then I was sent to St Peter's School, Gainford, County Durham, a home for Catholic Boys; it was also a breeding ground for crime. It was run by some sadistic nuns, or so they seemed to me; the worst of them were Irish, and how they hated us!

It was while I was in the workhouse that my granny died and I was told I would be going to St Peter's for three weeks - in fact I was there for five years. I was then ten years of age and entered St Peter's on September 10th 1928. I cried for about three weeks but no one was interested in why I was crying, the sisters just let me get it out of my system; then I began to settle down.

On entering the school I was introduced to my dormitory sister, Sister Anthony, who became like a real mother to me, but when I went up to the dormitory for the first time that night I got the shock of my life. All the boys were chattering and we were told to be quiet, but none of us took any notice until Sister Anthony grabbed three or four of the boys and gave them each six of the best over the hands with a cane. It

1

put the frighteners into me! Then I was shown my bed, shown how to fold my jersey and shorts up, where to put my shoes and socks under the bed and then get out into the ablutions which were outside the dormitory. We washed in cold water, showed ourselves to the sister and waited till we had passed inspection, then down on our knees on a highly polished floor covered by a huge cloth. We prayed and prayed, ten 'Hail Mary's' five times, then other prayers and after this we were sent to bed. It was lights out straight away and I lay and shivered in my bed; I imagined I was on the first stage to hell! In the morning we went through the same procedure except that prayers were shorter, and after them we went to the chapel in the school, for mass was three times per week when the local priest from Gainford came on Mondays, Wednesdays and Fridays. On top of this, we had mass on Sunday and Benediction in the afternoon of that day and on Tuesdays and Thursdays in the week.

I had my first communion there and that meant also my first confession. I had sinned, there is no doubt of that. I learned that everything except breathing was a sin! Each week we had to go to confession and it was expected that each time we went to mass we went also to communion. Suffice to say I was also confirmed at St Peter's; the Bishop of Hexham and Newcastle officiated. It didn't appear to make me any better. All I dreamed of was getting out of that home and seeing my mother.

My mother used to write to me at least once a week. I didn't always write back, for it wasn't any good asking her to take me home; I knew I didn't have one. There were about three hundred boys in the school who were in the same situation. I didn't like writing to my mum, not because I didn't want to tell her how I was doing, but because the letters we wrote were read out in class and the other lads laughed at what I put - mind you, I also laughed at what they put. I enjoyed school, especially Geography and History, essay-writing and Maths, but couldn't get on with Algebra. I just could not understand then, or now, how it could mean anything. I loved poetry, especially those about battles and men like Wellington. I also loved Shakespeare; I could recite whole pages from *The Tempest, Coriolanus*, and *As You Like It*. Singing at all times has given me the pip, but I love to hear good singing by people like Caruso and Mario Lanza. In school I lived in another world, which one day I was to see.

One day, in the very last days of December 1928, over a

2

hundred boys ran away. They were all brought back to the school; they were between thirteen and sixteen years old and too big to be caned. Although an enquiry was made into the matter, nothing came of it, but the man who was in charge of us in the playground during that day got his own back on us. It took some time until a certain day in early 1929. It was a bitterly cold winter that year and to keep warm we just huddled in corners of the playground or tried to play football with a tennis ball or an old 'tin block', that's an old tin can. Most of the boys came from the northern counties, that is, Northumberland, Durham, and Yorkshire, so football was in our blood; we even had Sammy Crooks of Derby County to coach us on one day each year. Anyway, to get back to this fiend in charge of us, his name was Morris and he had been a Northumberland Fusilier and I vowed that one day I would kill him.

This day, the playground began to get really slushy and to the playing field we went. The snow was well over a foot deep and he had us running around this field. It was big and windswept with no place to shelter and bitterly cold - it was so cold that our hair became full of frost. We had gone round the field about ten times when one of the bigger lads shouted out 'Shagger!' This made Morris seem to turn purple, I was near him and it was from our dormitory group that the voice had called out. He ran in front of us (there were about thirty boys in the group), halted us and asked who had called out. Naturally there was no reply, so he pulled everyone up and got our group together and marched us through the playground and into the 'Little Refectory', a small dining room for us lads of about eight to eleven years of age. We were then asked again who had called out this word, again no reply. We were then all threatened with the cane, so one of the big lads pushed a youngster of about ten, named Scott, forward. Morris had got someone to punish and he did! It seems unbelievable but he made us call out each strike he gave the lad, the cane being used was a drain rod with the metal ends removed. Poor old Scott got fifty lashes over the bare backside with this rod, then the same number on both hands; he was a hospital case really, he couldn't stand and bled from hands and buttocks. No one at school asked why Scott couldn't stand or use his hands. He was like it for three weeks. I can only think it must have been holiday time, or shortly after Christmas for it didn't impede Scott's schooling.

Our education was good, there is no doubt about that. We were taught how great our country was and that we should be proud to be

3

British. The best accolade, though, was if you were Irish. They were the ones who never did wrong and were treated like 'Holy Angels'. All our dormitories were called after saints; there were about forty-five boys per dormitory and in fact one of the dormitories was called 'Holy Angels'. I was in that one, but we weren't angels by any means. There were eight dormitories in all; we also had various annexes which were for 'old boys' if they should call, but none ever did while I was there.

We had a Roll of Honour for some thirty or more of the lads who had been killed in the Great War. We were rather proud of this. Little did we know that others in the not too distant future would be added.

In my first year at school, especially in the Refectory, I learned to look after Number One. You only had to look away from your plate and a slice of bread would disappear. At Christmas I lost a large 'gobstopper' through looking away; I never forgot that lesson and when called to look behind I always grabbed my food before I turned away.

Breakfast consisted of a pint mug of cocoa, and two slices of bread and marg. Dinner was either stew, or meat, potatoes and greens, followed by rice, sago (horrible stuff) or semolina usually nearly baked into a cake. Tea was as at breakfast. Those were our meals, the marg. nearly missed it was spread so thinly, but the bread was in 'clogs' (very thick slices).

Each day before we went to school we all had jobs to do, but to really explain how we did them I must set out the layout of the school. The buildings were set out in three sections from North to South and across and joining each set of buildings was a long passage of a hundred yards or so, this passage was completely covered and weather-proof. Looking at the school from the main road the left building consisted of six dormitories set in threes, and two were on top. The middle section between each dormitory was the washing area and bathroom plus a nun's bedroom and linen store. In the middle and below was the same set of rooms, while beneath was the school, but this was cut in two by the Little Refectory, the place where Scott had been so viciously attacked by the 'Minder' Morris.

The centre block from North to South again held the entrance, the nuns' Recreation Rooms, the stores and large Refectory. The centre passage cut the Refectory from these apartments, the third building at the end of the centre passage consisted of dormitories as before, but beneath was the chapel, workshop for the living-in carpenter/handyman and a huge playroom. This was the area in which we lived, and in the middle of the bottom section from the passage downwards was the playground, this was bounded by (1) the passage (2) the school and (3) the refectory. The end of the playground was contained by huge railings. No one was allowed outside these railings without permission.

At the left end of the playground was an open passage, this was about fifty yards long and led downhill to the nursery area where younger children were cared for. We saw little of this except if we were sent there to help with the cleaning, but this wasn't often. In the playground, Morris held sway!

On rising each morning at 7 a.m. we made our beds, washed, prayed and went to chapel. On the mornings we didn't go to chapel we scrubbed all the passages on our bare knees, swept all the dormitories and polished them, and by the time this was done it was breakfast time and immediately after, into school we went.

The people who had built and seen the buildings put up had done a really first class job. The walls were of red brick and looked a treat after rain. The entrance to the school was from a small gate on the main road through a well-planted area of ornamental trees and shrubs and just before reaching the main doors there was a statue of the Virgin Mary of The Immaculate Conception. This was how it was in 1928 when I was ten years of age.

The nuns were from the Order of St Vincent De Paul; they wore long, heavy, blue habits, with a white sort of skull cap which hid all their hair and this was crowned by a large white head-dress which gave the impression of swans on the wing. Around the waist they had a blue girdle and from this hung a very long rosary; usually as they walked along they were telling their beads (praying). Their chests were covered by large white bibs which ended almost at their waists. The usual procedure for the nuns was to visit the playground at least once an hour. They did nothing but just looked around. At the bottom of the playground was about a hundred yards of wasteland, this was the dumping ground for ashes from the school boiler which was nearby - the school was centrally heated even in those days! Looking across the wasteland there was a long wall eight feet high, and behind this was a huge garden from which all the vegetables for the school came. To the right of this was the football field and at the bottom of that was grassland and the River Tees.

To the right of the football field was the farm run by a couple of Irishmen. We had a herd of cows and several acres of ploughed land, usually root crops were grown there i.e. mangolds, turnips and carrots. I did the weeding there one day and couldn't distinguish carrots from weeds. The result was that I got a boot up my backside from the taller of the two Irishmen, whom we called 'Snipe' because of his long nose. His nose always dripped; he seemed to have a permanent cold. Milk from the farm was collected and the jam made by the nuns was sold; they filled huge earthenware jars with raspberry and strawberry jams and sealed these jars with mutton fat. I know, for I had to help to do this now and again.

One thing that stands out more than most things at the school was that I cannot remember at any time ever having had a cold, either runny nose or chest cold - we appeared to be immune. I think that this was due to the fact that all year round we kept the same clothing, shoes, socks, shirt (no vest) and a jersey, we certainly did not wear a hat. On top of this we were dosed every week with a small glass of Epsom Salts. There was no way of getting out of it, we had to queue to get this prior to going to bed and to make certain that we had drunk the potion we had to say 'thank you'. I can laugh at it now, but believe me it was no fun, especially next day when we all had the 'runs' and our toilets were in the school yard. There were no doors on them either, and did we have to shove and push to get seated?

We were exceptionally modest when we bathed, we had to keep a small towel round our waists when we got into the water and two lads had to hold up a sheet when we got out. Towels were communal and getting dry was a job. I think this was really false modesty, or perhaps we had to do this so that the nun in charge did not get excited on seeing our 'winkles'.

Well, all in all, it was a lousy time, but it was broken at intervals by long walks to Darlington (eight miles) and Barnard Castle, the same distance away from the school. We also went to the seaside once a year, either to Redcar or Saltburn. We drove the shopkeepers wild, I am certain, for we stole from them 'something awful'. Three or four of us

6

would go into a shop and ask for something that was at the back or up a ladder and, while the assistant was out of the way, we swiped anything at hand, sweets, gloves, toys etc. We always knew when a shop had been visited prior to our arrival for the shopkeepers chased us out before we had a chance to ask for anything. Well we never did get any money to spend. Usually we were dumped on the sands and told to be back at the dropping-off point round about 4 p.m. We then got on the bus and got a meal when we got back to school. We all enjoyed these trips, especially the sweets we gobbled up.

I suppose it doesn't sound too bad in the school, but it was really hell on earth. Some of the nuns, or sisters, were real sadists and some were very good, about two out of eighteen or more. They were Sisters of Charity all right, at the end of a cane or the back of their hands! It wasn't our fault we had been brought into the world and certainly not our fault we had been deprived of our homes. No matter how lowly a home is, it has a mother. Some are good, some are bad, but at least there is someone around you can tell your troubles to; there was no one like this at the school. I did have Sister Anthony, but you can't go telling tales, it's just not done. We were punished for the slightest infraction of the rules and that was it; there was no grey area.

One Christmas my mother sent me a Hornby train set. I saw it, but I was never allowed to play with it. It was put in the nuns' room; maybe it brightened up their lives, they were in prison really, while we were in captivity. No presents were given to us by the school and we didn't get turkey for dinner, of that I am sure. We did get plum pudding but we did not find sixpences in it. We had a lot of prayers and more prayers; it didn't do me much good, for all the kneeling and upping and downing got on my wick.

Most of the time I was a real dreamer. I used to think of Newcastle and all its bustle, the horse trams over the High Level Bridge, the Quay on Sunday and the Town Moor and Newcastle United and Hughie Gallagher the 'Wee Scots Lad' who was the pride of Tyneside. I'd think of when I used to go to Central Station at Newcastle and carry bags for passengers off the trains. Sometimes I even had enough to take home to my gran, for she had no money to spare, but I always tried to save sixpence for the football - it's a way of life in the North East.

Sitting in the playground at the school I thought of the times I had at Newcastle, especially in the winter. We once built a wall of snow across the street; it froze overnight and workmen had to bring picks next morning to take it down. We couldn't do anything like this at school, even snowballing was frowned upon.

My mother and my grandmother

I left the classroom when I was about fourteen years and six months old and was put to work in the garden which I enjoyed very much. I was also taught how to go shopping. I went on several errands for the school, ordering coal etc., and taking letters to the local priest, Father Dent. He was the one who came three or four times a week to the school to hear our confessions; we were all frightened of him, why, I don't know. He knew from what he told me that my mother had come from a fairly wealthy family, had been married at St Chad's Church of England Church, Gateshead, and after her marriage had embraced the Roman Catholic faith. As a result she had been cut off from the rest of the family and this had affected my gran as well. So much for bigotry!

Just before I was to leave the school, my mother came to see me. I would have been about five feet tall by then and very thin. I cannot remember what we talked about, but she left in tears. She had no place for me; she was still in service earning about £30 per year and she could not get a place of her own. This was in 1932 and I did not see her again until 1937.

I was called one day to the head office at the school; my fate was sealed! I was informed that I was to leave the school next day and go to St Mary's Abbey, East Bergholt, Suffolk. I knew where Suffolk was on the map, that was all; I was not told what I was going there for.

Prior to leaving the school I was issued with a suitcase, two shirts, two pants, two pairs of socks, one pair of shoes, a pullover, one tie and an overcoat. That was my lot and I was given one shilling to spend. Sister Anthony was to accompany me to London and then put me on the train to a place called Manningtree. Where that was I didn't know. Of course I know now, but then it was a voyage of discovery, as if I was going to the moon.

On the day I was leaving the school I found that I had a suit and that I was to wear long trousers. I was grown up! Hurray! I thought to myself 'I'm a man, look out, here I come'. Little did I know what was in store for me.

After a bus journey to Darlington, along with Sister Anthony, we boarded the train for London. I remember passing the engine of the train, it seemed like a monster dragon to me with it's hissing and groaning, I was both frightened and thrilled, it seemed like a real adventure. I was going on an adventure I suppose, and that hasn't finished yet.

I remember dodging away from my 'keeper' and getting a packet of Woodbines, they were then ten for fourpence, and Sister Anthony couldn't understand why I kept running to the toilet on our way South. I think she eventually got the message, for long before we got to London I was sick, (oh boy was I sick!) I looked like death warmed up. I got rid of the smokes before I left the train and vowed not to smoke ever again; this vow I was soon to break. Anyway we got to London and I had another fright. We went by Underground to Liverpool Street Station where I was put on a train, given a hug and a kiss by Sister Anthony and away I went, looking out of the carriage window all the way - I didn't want to miss my station.

Chapter 2 - The Abbey and the Army

I eventually arrived at Manningtree. I got off the train like a rocket and was met by an elderly man (he certainly was no gentleman, I soon learned), who introduced himself as the Captain. He took me to the Abbey at East Bergholt. This was on 13th October 1933.

After leaving Manningtree Station we had about three or four miles to go to the Abbey. It was pitch dark, but I saw that I had gone through some very high doors which led into a large open area. I learned next day that this was the farmyard of the Abbey and across this yard was a cottage and lean-to shed. We went into the cottage and were met by a lad I had known at the school - his name I remember was Smith. He greeted me not very enthusiastically, for we had not been friends and I had fought him many times and held my own against him; he was a bit of a bully. I couldn't have cared less but it didn't do much to endear me to the Captain and as soon as he saw that we knew each other and had had a talk with Smith, my name was mud!

The cottage consisted of a downstairs room and a kitchen, and three bedrooms upstairs. I was put into one of the upstairs rooms and when I awoke in the morning, having been called at 6 a.m. by the Captain, I found that my window looked out on to a graveyard. It didn't worry me, but I thought what a lonely place it was - there were no flowers and no headstones on the graves, just mounds.

I soon found out what I had to do. I was taken to the Mother Superior and introduced, and found that I was to be at their beck and call, their communication with the outside world. No other person was allowed into that part of the Abbey. The nuns there belonged to the Order of St Benedict and wore black from head to foot. I used to chop their wood, clean the chicken houses, dig the garden, get the milk, all little chores which I didn't mind. I used to get into trouble with the Captain, he being our boss, because I used to swipe all the willow wood I could find. It was easy to chop and when you have a week's supply to get ready it's a bit much if it's hard and gnarled.

It didn't suit the Captain that the nuns always wanted me to run little errands in the village for them, like getting stamps and sometimes

The Abbey at East Bergholt

bread, or taking their flat black shoes to the cobblers; I think he was a little jealous. I had to serve at Mass each day for them as well and met all manner of reverend gentlemen. The one in charge at the Abbey was Friar Sibley; he was a grand old man.

I suppose there were about sixty nuns at the Abbey and they certainly worked hard, for although I dug parts of their garden at times, the main work was done by them; I was really only a little boy. Each day I had to take their milk from the farm to them and each day I was given a pint of hot milk to drink. I hated it but drank it, I didn't like up-setting the nun in the kitchen for she always had a nice hot slice of toast for me each morning I called. At Christmas I got all manner of presents, ties, shirts and socks; I really did well, and everything fitted me.

I wasn't in any way embarrassed being amongst the nuns for one of the jobs I had done at the school was clearing away the tables from the sisters' Refectory and helping them to wash up.

I learnt a lot of country ways while I was at the Abbey. We had several acres and on Saturday I used to go poaching with one of the farm hands. I didn't know it was poaching until one day I had shot a rabbit and a bellow came from across the field we were in and my companion told me to run. All I knew then was that we were doing something wrong; the best of it was that we had set snares all over the place. Anyway, we got out of it and I asked why the man had bellowed

11

like that and was told it was his field. We sold what rabbits we had got for a shilling each which made our money up. I was at that time receiving three shillings per week and 'living in' as the saying is.

The Captain had been told by Smith of our escapade and he tried to hit me round the ear. I ducked, he missed and I framed up to him. He didn't try any more, ever, but in his sneaky way tried to get round me, tucking me into bed and trying to get his hand down the bed, I enlightened him and told him in no uncertain terms to keep out of my way. I was growing up!

The Abbey at East Bergholt was opposite the Church of England Church. It was a peculiar church, for the bells were in a big cage in the grounds and not in the tower. I learned of the village's famous son, John Constable, the Abbey being at the head of Dedham Vale close to Flatford Mill, the spot which Constable had made famous by his paintings, but of course at that time it didn't mean anything to me.

Christmas came and went at the Abbey with all its religious cere-monies, and it got bitterly cold. It was literally like an ice-house where we lived in the cottage. The Captain didn't make matters easier, he was always yakking about his connection with Toc H or some such organisation - he had been a friend of the founder. There was nowhere to go, so I usually went to bed and by candlelight read as much as I could. We buried one nun who died - such a simple affair, taking no more than a few minutes to launch her off to the 'great beyond'.

One day, when I was nearly sixteen, I heard that rotten Captain talking about me to Smith. He was saying that as soon as I was sixteen the nuns would not pay my National Insurance stamp and 'He'll have to look for another job, he can't be kept here', and that was the beginning of the end of my life at St Mary's Abbey and East Bergholt in Suffolk.

Next day I took off. I went to Ipswich and, as I had always been keen on soldiers, I found a recruiting office and asked if I could join the Royal Artillery. I don't remember the reply I got, but I had visions of riding a horse, blowing a trumpet and firing the guns - just up my street! I had no idea that you could get killed in the process and I didn't realise that to be a soldier you had to be trained. I thought you just joined - what shocks I was to get!

Anyway, in a letter I was informed that there were no vacancies in the Royal Artillery but there were some in the Norfolk Regiment and I could join as a bandboy. Bang went my ideas of charging across the prairie, sword in hand, dealing out death and destruction to all and sundry.

To cut a long story short I said I would like to join the army and duly reported at Ipswich Recruiting Centre where I was sworn in and received the King's Shilling. I was given a railway warrant to London and was told to make my way to Waterloo Station where I would be met by a Sergeant, which I did, and I was given another warrant to Devonport where the Norfolk Regiment 2nd Battalion was stationed at South Raglan Barracks.

In due course I arrived at the barracks and reported to the Guard Room and eventually to Band Master E.C.H.Burgess, who informed me that I would be taught to play a musical instrument. In fact it was the trombone. I was then taken to the 'Boys Room' in Headquarter Company. Naturally upon arrival I was the object of intense interest. Someone had informed the 'Boys' that I was a trombone virtuoso, which was light years away from the truth. I informed them of that fact amid a great deal of laughter and I always remember some wag who asked 'I wonder who dropped this bollock'. There were some sixteen boys; we were either 'drums' or 'band'. A corporal named 'Jock' Milne was in charge and he really did look after us like a mother hen. He was a really good sort.

I was allocated a bedcot, two sheets, three 2' square biscuits, three blankets, pillow-case and pillow, plus a kit box. I was shown how to make up my bed, how to fold it up and told that that area of the room was mine and to make sure that I kept it clean and didn't leave my kit (of which I had none at the time) all over the place or I would lose it! I must explain that the bedding biscuits were made of coir, hard and stiff; they had to be because when our beds were not in use we had to fold the blankets round them, one lay flat and the other two stood to attention, the odd blanket, sheets and pillow folded behind.

The barrack room where the 'boys' were was about fifty feet by twenty feet with painted walls; the top was cream and the bottom dark brown and a one inch line divided the two. There were about twenty bedcots in the room, ten each side and in the far right corner was the bunk of our corporal in charge. Each cot was 6' 6" long when fully extended and it was made completely of steel, three 6" slats forming the base. When the beds were not in use the front half of the cot was pushed back to go under the back half, there were eight legs to support it. On top of this was put the neatly folded blankets and coir biscuits and this we used as a chair. In the middle of the room was a bare deal table on iron legs and two forms which were 8' long. There was also a large steel coal bunker in the room, together with a highly-polished, silvery blue steel bucket which was about 18" across at the top and could be carried by two handles at each side, this was used as a waste bin and also to carry our coal from the issuing lorry some three flights of stairs from our room. Each one of us had a job, dusting or polishing, the latter being worse, for that could not be done until everyone had tidied round his bedcot and swept up. In time I was allocated the job of polishing the floor which was bare and dark stained, but it shone like a mirror. We had the room inspected daily by our Corporal, then by the Band Sergeant and frequently by the Company Sergeant Major.

Above the bed we kept our equipment; this consisted of pack, haversack, respirator and steel helmet, all packed on top of each other with a box inside to keep them square and neat. On the right side stood our water bottle, on the left our mess tin. In front of the shelf and secured to it was our number plate, of polished brass which gave our regiment, name and number. Below the shelf, on the centre peg of three, was our great-coat with the front facing the wall. On the outside pegs hung our webbing equipment consisting of belt, two ammo pouches, straps and bayonet frog or holder - being under eighteen we did not have rifles or bayonets.

The day after I arrived at South Raglan Barracks I was issued with my kit. Being the 18th February this was a great day in the annals of the Regiment, 'Shaiba' Day. The Battalion trooped the colour and took the rest of the day off (they were half dead after it anyway). This was a battle honour from the 1914-1918 War when some glorious deed had been performed in Mesopotamia; what it was I couldn't tell you, I never did find out in all my service years.

Getting my kit was a gas, no measuring up, the Company Quarter Master Sergeant looked at me then gave me two vests, two jackets, two sets of puttees, two caps (one a fatigue hat) canvas uniform, two pairs of boots, three pairs of socks, two pairs of trousers and a great-coat, along with a knife, fork and spoon, razor, comb and lather brush, gloves, two towels, and sets of badges and numerals for my jackets and coat. These were all bundled into a kit bag and I was fitted out, with the warning not to 'bloody well be here tomorrow saying you have lost anything, you won't get the bugger'.

The badge of the Norfolk Regiment at that time was a Britannia surrounded by laurel leaves and the name of the Regiment underneath; the collar badges were a plain Britannia holding out a laurel branch. On the shoulder we wore the word 'NORFOLK'.

The first thing I had to do when I got back to the barrack room was sort this lot out, take all the buttons off my tunic and put on regimental ones, two for my shoulder straps, four for my breast pockets and side pockets and five big buttons for the front of my tunic, eleven in all. Then came my great-coat, two for the shoulder straps, three for the back belt, two at the bottom coat-tail and five large buttons in the front. Quite a job, but all the lads mucked in and the job was soon done. Having completed this task, it now came to the disposal of my civilian clothes. I was informed by our room corporal that I must get rid of it, so the lads came and either paid me or I gave away the lot. Little did I know what a fool I was in doing this, but I had been told to send the lot home and I didn't have one, so what could I do? What I should have done was parcel them up and put them away in my kit box. Still, it was no loss for I soon grew out of everything. By the time I was eighteen years of age I was six feet one and a half inches tall. I was only five feet one inch when I joined; all this growing took place in two years.

I can remember each and every one of those boys. All are dead now, either killed in the 1939-1945 War in France or in Burma or Singapore. What a loss, for they were the salt of the earth. All or nearly all came from Norfolk - I think of them often and thank heaven how lucky I am.

Each day we had Reveille at 7 a.m. and were on parade for P.T. at 7.30 a.m., down to the gym till 8.15 a.m. and then to breakfast and on parade for band practice at 9 a.m. We polished all our buttons etc. each night and put them under our blankets to keep clean. We were always up before the bugle-call. It didn't do us much harm, but we had a P.T. Instructor who was a real bastard. After the P.T. was over he would shout out 'Dismiss' at which we had to turn smartly right, rise on our toes and buzz off. Every time we did it with him we were always called back to do the drill again. He used to ask one of us, we all had a turn, to shake hands and on putting your right hand out he used to belt us one in the stomach and laugh; we couldn't get away from it for he made it an order, but we knew what was coming and used to fall back so we didn't feel the full force of the blow.

15

One day during the regimental boxing, he met a young recruit called Miller straight from the Depot at Norwich. They were fighting as heavyweights and this lad was considered to have no chance. While the fight was on we yelled and yelled for this lad and screamed our heads off when our tormentor went down for good, for this recruit flattened our bullying P.T.I. and gave him an almighty hiding. From that day on the corporal was a changed man,

One thing that really got up our noses with our P.T.I. was him asking for a cigarette, crafty in a way for he didn't ask too often, but now and again one of us would offer him one. We would be all dressed in our full uniform by the time he asked us and when the cigarette was proffered he would take it, then have us all tip our pockets out and collect all the cigs we had. We were fairly wise to this game of his but there was always someone who got caught. We weren't allowed to smoke, being on 'Boy Service'. Everyone knew that we did. but he always made sure that we should understand that it was forbidden - at least he didn't put us on a charge.

Our lives consisted of drill, band practice morning and afternoons, equipment cleaning and P.T. It wasn't a bad life and I soon fell into the swing of it. Our pay was seven shillings per week and after three months service we got ten shillings per month uniform allowance. Keeping our uniforms clean, besides being a matter of pride, was also a matter of saving up, for we got two shillings in hand each pay day which was a Friday; we went up to the officer at the pay table, were given the two shillings and said 'Thank You'; five shillings went into credit, and if we wanted more we used to put a chit in for the amount we needed and that was called a 'mark up'.

The idea was, I suppose, to make me a musician and a soldier. I became the latter and was fairly competent on the second trombone, but while we were boys, other than when practising with the full band, we were only allowed to play long notes and scales, running, melodic and diatonic. We got a further extra hour if caught having a go at a march or any other piece of music. We also learned the meaning of musical terms. One I will never forget is *pesante*, which means heavily. I was asked a score of times about this term and I would forget, but one of our corporals who was taking us 'young hands' found a novel but hurtful way to remind me. He gave me a whack on the back of the head with a music lead, which is a piece of steel some twelve inches long and a half inch wide to hold down the music when playing a concert in the open. A few taps and at last I knew what the term meant!

Band practice each day except Saturday and Sunday was 9 a.m. - 12 noon and for us boys it was also 2 p.m. - 3 p.m. daily. Besides this we had to drill and do fatigues, i.e. cleaning the barrack area, cook house duty and mess hall duty. We were free all Saturday and Sunday and from 5 p.m. daily except if we were in 'defaulters' having got C.B. (confined to barracks) for any manner of offences such as long hair, puttee tapes showing, dirty instrument, buttons or equipment. Sometimes we would hear of a man getting 'Aldershot'; that meant he had been court-martialled for a serious military offence such as desertion or striking an N.C.O. Three and seven days were the usual punishments and the bugler sounded defaulters at 7 a.m. then at 1 p.m. making certain that no one was absent. Those excused the call were either on guard or away on some detail or other. At 5 p.m. and every hour thereafter, on the hour, the call went and it had to be answered, this went on till Last Post at night and next day it all began again. During the period anyone was on defaulters, commonly known as 'Jankers', all manner of fatigues were done, whitewashing stones, cookhouse duty, cell-cleaning and anything that came under the Provost Sergeant's eye that needed doing or he thought up.

I had two great friends in the band, brothers George and Joseph Green; we always went out together and as far as I know George is still alive, but Joe was later killed in France.

Besides our band duties all bandsmen had to learn First Aid, I was attached to 'D' company for this but that was only on paper, for it was not till war broke out that we really went to our companies.

Now, the band and drums were two different sections in Headquarter Company. We, the band, had a W.O. Class 1 in charge, while the drums have an N.C.O. in the person of a Drum Major, a rank equal to a sergeant in a line company. The B.M. is an appointed rank, has been a student at the Military School of Music, Kneller Hall, Twickenham, while the D.M. has risen from the ranks. The B.M. usually has L.R.A.M. and A.R.C.M. after his name. Ours hadn't but he was up to his job.

We had khaki uniform for normal parades, but for Officers' Mess Nights and playing in parks etc., we wore flat blue hats, red tunics with yellow neck-bands and cuffs, in other words the colours of our regiment,

Band and Drums, 2nd Battalion, The Royal Norfolk Regiment.
Trombones centre back row - the author 7th from the right

red, yellow and black. Our footwear was either shoes or boots, the latter being normal for in those days not many of us could afford shoes.

Besides wearing our khaki uniform we also, as did all troops in those days, wore box-creased trousers. This box crease was made by turning the leg of the trousers from one hand's breadth below the knee inside out and pressing it razor sharp, then, to put the trousers on, the crease was released to boot top then folded in below the knee, the bottom tucked into the sock of the leg, then a puttee was wound round the leg. This was some fifteen feet long and had to end exactly on the left or right of the leg; the trouser was then turned down. If the puttee tape showed, it was a certain three days, for you were improperly dressed. Puttees are laughed at nowadays, but they were good, for they kept the legs warm and if put on correctly were very smart.

With the uniform we wore white buckskin belts, the usual brass attachments for fastening and a card case, this was slung across the left shoulder and held tight there by the shoulder strap and a buckle of brass. The card case fitted across the back, was about six inches by ten inches and showed a large Britannia badge on a circular yellow cloth background. Both belt and case were white blancoed.

The Drum Section consisted of drums, tenor and side flutes, and bugles. The uniform was exactly as ours, but their duties were slightly different in that they did not belong to the stretcher-bearing squads but to the Intelligence Section! Believe me there were some real bright sparks in that lot! Usually they ended up as Company Runners - well someone had to do the job. They were never considered as prospective candidates for the R.M.S.M. Kneller Hall, come to that neither was I, for although I didn't mind being in the band I just wasn't a real soldier and that's what I wanted to be. It took years to get my wish.

While at South Raglan Barracks we had an influx of boys into our Section from Watts Naval School, North Elmham, Norfolk, a branch of Doctor Barnardo's Homes. They weren't a bad lot really, but rough, tough and well able to look after themselves in more ways than one, especially at scrounging, not stealing, but any soldier will tell you what scrounging means and these lads were well versed in that.

One, a lad called Tim Wittems, was a really big chap, about six feet three inches tall when he joined. He pinched my boot brushes one day and when I claimed them back he clumped me round the ear for my trouble; the brushes were mine alright but he had 'made' them. I couldn't fight him back, he was so huge, so I cut my losses and forgot about the matter. Wittems eventually became heavyweight boxing champion of the Regiment.

The Regiment stayed some two years at South Raglan Barracks and we had a good time both in Devenport and Plymouth, both Navy towns. We used to go to 'Aggie Westons'; this was like the Salvation Army, or Church Army. They were dead against drink and each time we went there we signed 'the Pledge' swearing not to drink intoxicating liquor. I must have signed ten times in all. We usually got a sermon after this but best of all we got a free feed, cakes and pies etc. - that's all we went for anyway.

From Devonport we went to Mandora Barracks, Aldershot. The N.C.Os thought this wonderful, home of the British Army etc., but the officers must have begun to get the wind up, no more gadding about at social events, at least not so much of it. We knew things were going to alter for we had hours of extra drill and parades. I suppose it was decided that we had been having a lazy time in Devonport, but we hadn't really.

From Devonport we used to march, with our C.O. a Colonel Shand, followed by Major 'Footy' Reynolds on horseback, to Fort Tregantle where field firing exercises were carried out. This wasn't really a fort but a large collection of barrack huts situated on top of the cliffs overlooking Plymouth Sound. It was a good place, but we weren't allowed to go swimming because several persons had drowned in the area.

Along with us on the march we had a cookwagon; this was pulled by two horses and food was cooked in it en route. It was supposed to be able to feed the battalion on the move, but all we ever got from it was hot tea. Still, give a soldier a mug of tea and he'll march for days. All the rest of the battalion's kit came on limbers drawn by horses. I reckon that's what we went to Aldershot for, to be re-equipped, for in truth we were still the 1914-18 army; we had Lee Enfield Rifles Mark IV, Lewis Guns and Vickers Heavy Machine Guns. 'A' Company, who were known as Machine Gun Company, did a lot of 'schemes' at Tregantle, all withdrawals; it is no wonder that in later years the army did so badly in France - we hadn't been taught anything about attack and advance.

At no time while at Tregantle did I fire any weapon because we were too young, but we had to mark in the butts. We learned a trick or two there I can tell you. What we did I will tell you later, but it all had to do with an ordinary pencil and a .303 bullet.

Mandora Barracks at Aldershot is situated between Buller Barracks and the Cambridge Hospital, Buller being the Depot of the R.A.S.C. and Catering Corps, and the Cambridge being run by the R.A.M.C. whose Depot was at Crookham, not far from Aldershot.

There were the normal roads running through the barracks, plus playing fields, and Maida Vale Gym was not far away. We went to the gym five days a week, either running or marching about a mile. By 10 a.m. we would be back to our normal duties, either band practice or Drum Major's instructions on Bugle Calls etc. There were no parades on Saturdays after 12 noon.

The calls we had to learn were as follows :-

Reveille   - Get out of bed you lazy buggers, get out of bed.

Jankers - You'll be on jankers as long as you like as long as you answer the call.

Meals - Come to the cookhouse door boys, come to the cookhouse door, the bread is on the table, the meat is on the floor.

Company Call - Fall in A, Fall in B, Fall in all the Company. This was followed by one long 'G' for HQ Co. and two for A, three for B, and so on till D was reached.

Sick Call - Sixty four ninety four won't go sick again no more, the poor blighter is dead.

Alarm or Stand To- Get out and stand your ground, repeated some three times.

Retreat, Last Post were the main calls of the evening (jankers stood to attention outside the Guardroom at this call) and the last call of the day was 'Lights Out'. All calls were preceded by the Regimental Call which was worded so :- We are the Ninth of Foot, What Ho!

Reveille and Last Post, plus Retreat did not have this sounded before the main call.

I cannot remember the call for Advance, and cannot remember at any time in the pre-war Army that we ever practised this, we did nothing but 'strategic withdrawals'.

By this time I was a full-blown Bandsman, and I marched and played with the band on all parades and at Officers Mess. Discipline was very strict. I can remember one night after playing 'The King' the C.O. came yelling at the rear of me 'Bandmaster, Bandmaster look at this man, he stood at ease during 'The King' put him on a charge'. I suppose my feet or heels were about two inches apart; I looked down and couldn't believe what I had heard. Anyway, to cut a long story short I feigned a bad knee and got away with it. No wonder Officers Mess call was 'Officers Wives get pudding and pies and we poor buggers get skilly'.

While at Mandora our boy's team got into the fifth round of the Army Cup, we were no hot shots or anything like that, but we had some good games. In one game I was nearly sent off; it took place like this.

I normally played left half, this being football you understand, and this day we were playing the West Yorks, a big burly lot whom we had never beaten because of a great lumbering ox of a lad who played right back for them. He was literally flattening our lot and I was getting browned off at this so I swapped with the left wing of our side and came up against this lad. He was coming at me as I went ahead, like an express train, so, just before he got to me to charge me over, I dropped my left shoulder, bent down slightly and lifted myself up with a jerk, over my head he went, his momentum really doing the job for me. The next thing I knew was that the whistle had blown. I got a good telling off, but after that the game went on quite well and we won.

Another game I had was at Farnborough against the Cameron Highlanders. They were really good and had always beaten us as they did on this day, but I scored the best goal of my life against them. Running down the left wing I belted it over and it shot like a bullet into the back of the net. There was only one snag, we didn't have any spectators. I thought, all that and no cheers, what a swizz!

The most jammy goal I ever scored was again against the Camerons. It was bitterly cold and windy and I had hardly had a kick, so when the ball came to me just inside the Cameron half, I just belted the ball and it flew into the air, down the pitch and into the back of the net. We won, and no one was more surprised than I, but our Company Commander a Major Brorne, refused to give me the shilling he always gave to the goal-scorers on our side. He told me I didn't deserve it and I should pay him the shilling. Still I hung around him and he relented, giving me the shilling I didn't really have a right to, such a lousy game I had played, and I knew it.

There was plenty of sport at Aldershot, but football was my forte. I played hockey and basket-ball and there was swimming as well, but I was scared stiff then of the water. I learned better later.

During July and August of 1936 we went on Grand Manoeuvres and marched till nearly on our chin straps. Bren gun and Bren gun carriers, and small lorries had been issued to us, but the lorries weren't there to ride in, we still went by Shanks Pony and marched from Aldershot to a huge camp at Petworth in Sussex. Getting there I had my first laugh over the call 'Get out with your feet'; this meant we had a foot inspection after our long march. I always had a good laugh at this call, we all did, it sounded so daft. Never once during my army service did I ever have a foot blister - there are not many who can say that.

We marched at night looking for tanks, but I don't believe there were any, for we didn't see them; all we saw was fields and more fields, Bren gun carriers and officers with flags telling us we were dead. We always tried to get captured, for this meant we went straight back to camp and lazed about till the exercise was over, or cleaned our kit or had a kip. But back in camp we usually got into trouble. One of our lads got eight days glasshouse for a prank. We had got back to camp and all our kit was outside and the tent flaps rolled up bar one. There was a bulge in the tent, so this blighter got a mallet and gave the bulge a real wallop. Unfortunately it turned out to be an N.C.O's head! Our lad was arrested and given eight days detention by the C.O. for this.

We were still at camp when our friend returned; his equipment was whiter than white and his hair was about half an inch in length. His eight days away had really knocked the stuffing out of him. On nearing the glasshouse he had tried to make a run for it, but the N.C.O. escort had tapped him on the head with his cane, which was loaded with lead and he could not remember how he entered the detention cells. This chap was killed in France later; I think he won the Military Medal for bravery, a real cockney from Shoreditch.

It was while we were at this camp on Grand Manoeuvres that a reporter from the Eastern Daily Press visited us; he gave the Regiment a great 'write-up' - I remember it plainly. He told how about eight hundred of us men were fed in half an hour by our 'magnificent cooks'. We were dumbfounded on reading this. We had had several copies of the E.D.P. sent so that we could read about it. What it didn't say was that what had been 'cooked' were eight hundred *tins* of stew! The cans were holed then put into dixies, boiled and one given to each man. Actually what we got was fat and greasy meat with carrots and potatoes mixed. It made good reading for the public anyway. Normally meals would have taken some four hours to prepare and serve.

By this time it must be understood that I had left 'Boy Service'. I now got 15s.9d. per week, for whilst I had been on Boy Service I had passed my first, second and third Educational Exams. Basic pay was 14s. per week and the 1s.9d. was for having passed my third exam.

After two years I also had a 'hard hitter' on my left sleeve (one good conduct badge) and above that I had L.G. and crossed guns to show that I was a marksman in both weapons. The L.G. was the Lewis Gun, the worst weapon ever invented for automatic firing because it had so many stoppages. The slightest dent in the mag. stopped it from being rotated when fired. The day we got the Bren certainly cured a lot of loss of pay to many men, it was so easy to fire and to carry.

We went to Ash and Bisley Ranges for firing practice with rifle, Bren and for A Coy. (Machine Gun Coy.) the heavy Vickers Machine Gun. The best job was in the butts, the targets were on pulleys or stands which went up and down after each man had fired, we gave the usual marking signals, by means of a large round disc on a pole and had white one side and black the other, much as it is now. No telescopes were allowed. The marking went as follows:- white disc in the centre for a 'bull', black disc across the target for an inner, a twirled disc for a magpie, and an outer, the black disc was moved up and down the target with black to the front, a miss or 'scrubber' was denoted by a red and white flag. The target was actually some five feet square and was fired at from 500, 400, 300, 200, and 100 yards, in one exercise we fired at all ranges, this was called the 'long advance'. I once hit the target at this range myself. The target was split into four sections, the centre about one foot wide was the bull and was black, then a further circle outward was the inner, then the 'magpie' and then the outer circle. We always knew when the target was hit by the crack as the bullet went through, a miss you didn't hear, but saw a cloud of dust either above, below or at either side.

It wasn't very often that a man lost his pay on the range for we always knew who was firing. We were in communication with the firing points by field phone and if one of our mates missed we used to shoot up a 'bull' and eventually when he had finished firing and we went to clean the target by pasting over the holes, we shot a pencil through the paper of the target and this was exactly as if a bullet had passed through. Many a man was declared a 'sniper' having earned this title through a pencil. He may have been the worst shot in the platoon. Getting caught was a certain fourteen days but no one in our section ever did. We all got our pay, 14s. basic, 1s.9d. Educational and 1s.9d. for being a First Class Shot, in all 17s.6d. per week.

One fine day there were rumours that we were going to Palestine, we were all inoculated and vaccinated and had our kits made up, then we marched down to the military siding at Aldershot, looked at the train and marched back. We didn't go anywhere! This was a good thing for there was trouble in Palestine and no one wanted to go in any case.

Things went on as usual, but in due course I ended up with an abscess in my right ear and went to the Cambridge Hospital which was near our barracks. I was put to bed and eventually was seen by a doctor, but before he came in we were subject to the biggest bit of army bull there could be. The ward sister shouted out 'Lie to attention!' I dread to think of what would have taken place had any of us been on a bedpan!

One night I was sitting on my bedcot cleaning my equipment, doing the brasses in fact, when a voice said 'Are you getting ready for inspection?' I didn't take much notice and the voice said 'Are you ready for the Great Inspection?' Hearing this and not looking up, I replied that we'd had Generals Inspection last week and that was enough. I looked up and saw a young man with two black pips on his shoulders and realised that he must be a priest or parson. In fact he was neither, he belonged to the Church Army. He then asked if I was ready for the Great Inspection, ready to meet my maker. I had a blue fit and asked him if *he* was and to leave me alone. He did, in fact, and never spoke to anyone else in the room. I reckon if I was a specimen of the men in our barrack room we weren't worth saving, but there's a time and place for everything.

In the barrack room I slept near to our Room Corporal, Paddy McCarthy, he was a really nice bloke, a saxaphone player, and each morning, knowing the cooks, he used to get up and get a mug of tea and invariably I got half, but one morning I went for the char. The mug was too full so he told me to drink it; I did, I drank the lot and a few minutes later he asked for his char. Well, he got out of bed, slammed me one round the ear and used every swear word in the book. I daren't answer back, but he didn't bear any grudges and next day we were sharing the char again. That's how it is in the army, you muck in, you have your rows and fights, but we were all brothers in what we did, we were soldiers, that's all.

Chapter 3. Gibraltar

At about 11a.m. just before we left Aldershot I was in the canteen having a 'char and wad' (tea and rock cake). This cost twopence, the cheapest you could get at the N.A.A.F.I. (No Aim, Ambition or Flaming Interest). There was no one in there and all the newspapers were at hand. I sat there awhile, then I went to the billiard table and had a couple of swipes at the balls, and then it hit me! I was due on parade with H.Q. Coy. to be inoculated and boy, did I run to the Company lines! There was the Company all formed up, Band, Signals, Armourers, the lot. The Sergeant Major greeted me with 'Thank you very much Mr Troup, I'm glad to see you are turning up today'. I gaped at him - the rest of the parade were laughing as you can imagine - and then out it came, 'You'll be on a bloody charge tomorrow. Be at Company Office at 9 a.m.' In due course I went to Company Office, got marched in 'Left right, left right'. The Sergeant Major yelled out the charge and I was asked if I had anything to say and when I began to speak I was ordered to 'Shut up, three days, march him out'.

On Jankers, I met the Provost Sergeant, Sgt. Dixie Dean. It was rare for a bandsman to get on Jankers and he didn't get me to scrub floors or kitchen duty; all I got was cleaning his belt and bayonet each day for the three days - a piece of cake. Dixie, as he was known to all and sundry, was a real friend and I never forgot his kindness to me. I kept in touch with him till he died aged 83 years; he was a real old soldier, a kindly man.

The day came when we had to leave Aldershot. Our band marched in sixes right across the road, the companies behind in threes or fours. Some of the bandsmen had been in the First World War, men named Stapleton, Dolman and Harris, the latter pair were Lance Corporals. Dolman was to my left in about the fourth rank behind the drums. I looked ahead and could see that a cover in the middle of the road was off right in front of Dolman. He was blowing away like mad, not looking at the music as he knew it off by heart, and instead of seeing the manhole he walked straight into it, went in like a dart. He didn't hurt himself but his trombone bent almost into a figure of eight. Well those who saw it stopped playing; we couldn't help it for laughing, but Dolman, when he returned to the ranks, didn't think much of us. Still it helped us along, for, except that we didn't have our rifles, we were like camels marching along. We had full Field Service Marching Order on which meant: pack filled with about 26 lbs of kit, ammo pouches less ammo, belt, bayonet, haversack and water bottle. On the pack we had our groundsheets, gas capes and steel helmets. Being in the band on the march was no fun I can tell you, the companies behind didn't have to blow like us - they didn't sing either. I've never heard soldiers sing on the march, or whistle either.

We eventually got to the military siding at Aldershot Railway Station, and soon we were off. To me it was a great adventure; I really was thrilled and looked forward to the voyage with wonder and excitement.

Upon arrival at Southampton I found that we were sailing on the *Lancashire*, a troopship which to all intents and purposes looked like an overgrown yacht. It was owned by the P.&.O. Line, painted all white with a blue line all round the ship at deck level; it had one funnel and this was coloured light brown. Any similarity to a yacht soon disappeared on boarding the ship. There were two main cargo holds, which contained the Regimental clutter; the rest of the ship below decks was our dining rooms, sleeping quarters and mess decks. There were about four of these areas on the ship. There were about twenty tables, twenty feet long, either side of the deck with benches either side of them. Above these tables were row upon row of hooks and above we stored

H.T.Lancashire
27

our greatcoats, boots and equipment. At each table was seating for twenty to thirty men, the first two seats at the table (I soon learned never to sit there again) were for the two mess orderlies who had to get the food, clean the tables and keep the area clean. Having arrived last for a place, I found I was allocated this job.

On getting to this deck area I thought to myself, 'where the devil do you sleep?' I soon learned, for there was a shout of 'Come and get your hammocks'. Then I learned where I was to sleep, yes! on those lousy hooks! When we eventually did get our hammocks slung, it looked like the inside of a sardine tin.

There is a certain smell about any ship, but a troopship takes the biscuit; it is a combination of sweaty bodies and feet, stale food and urinals.

On the other side of the dock at Southampton was the *Queen Mary*, then the largest ship afloat. I would have swapped places any day with the passengers aboard that liner. The *Queen Mary* was decked overall with bunting and we all came on deck when her hooter went, an extremely deep growl; with the little tugs edging her out, she was soon away and out of sight. When *we* left, there was no one other than the dockers to say goodbye, and we certainly didn't have any bunting flying.

The voyage to Gibraltar was without incident, for although the Spanish Civil War was at its height it was no concern of ours and we sailed merrily along for four or five days.

Up till we got to the Bay of Biscay I was O.K. and had a good laugh at those who were sick - little did I realise that my time was to come. I was coming down the companion way and hit my head on the door roof, nearly knocking myself out. I went to sleep on the floor that night, just as well as we ran into a storm and I was sick. I spent all night with my head over the side. That was the first and last time I was ever sick at sea and I have been on three long voyages.

We arrived quite safely at Gibraltar and docked in the Naval Harbour; there was one snag, the Cameron Highlanders, who we were relieving, were already on the dock. Our equipment and regimental stores had to come off and theirs had to come on. This went on all afternoon and, instead of stopping at night, carried on right through until about

6 a.m. the following day when we did finally get off. There were fights with the 'Jocks' - they called us 'Sassenach bastards' and we called them 'Burgu' (porridge-eating bastards). We never slept and were glad to be off the boat, and marching up to Buena Vista Barracks which was to be our future home. The Battalion was stationed either there or at North Front which was near the border fence with Spain, the border being closed.

Being stationed on the Rock in those days was a piece of cake. We didn't do much, a few drills and parades and from about 2 p.m. daily we either went out on the booze (everything was duty free) or swimming. It was in Gibraltar that I learned to swim; I was just eighteen and there were boys in our mob who could swim like fish. As for me, I lay either in the rocks or the sand and just looked on, till one day I decided that I'd had enough. There was a big rock jutting out some thirty feet into the sea where we swam, so I went to the end of it and jumped in, it must have been fifteen to twenty feet deep there, anyway I got ashore and tried and tried again and again and in the end I did swim. I learned very quickly and thoroughly enjoyed my dips in the sea. I could dive deep and took part in many a game of water polo. I couldn't understand why I hadn't learned before. With the sea and the sun we soon became as brown as berries.

As you can imagine, being eighteen I thought I was one of the lords of creation, proud to be in the army, proud of my Regiment and proud of myself and that I was British.

I suppose it was alright being proud, but in reality we were living in cloud cuckoo land. There was a war on in Spain but it didn't affect us much; we weren't allowed into Spain, at least the 'other ranks' weren't, and except for a few guards and parades life was really easy. We cleaned our rifles, webbing equipment and the like, the band played at Mess Nights for the Officers and that was it.

I have often thought of all the spit and polish and the brass cleaning that went on and now I wonder how many lives were lost over this bit of bull, over and over I think of that, and our webbing, both white and green. I am sure had we saved the blanco we could have used it on the Germans, sending a cloud of it over. What a dust storm that would have been!

On the Rock we didn't do much heavy training, but we 'Manned the Rock'. This was an exercise we all liked, for we all had various stations to go to. I was on Genista Battery. This was a seven-inch gun set in a strategic part of the Rock close to our barracks at Buena Vista. The gunners were all Royal Artillery who were stationed at Europa Point, the most southerly point in Europe. I was Ack Ack gunner with a Lewis Gun, of all the useless things, for the big gun hadn't been fired in living memory; it was alleged to have a cracked barrel, but how true this was we never knew.

The 'Manning' took two days. The alarm was sounded over the Rediffusion Service Radio, we ran and got our gun and away we went. On the day of one of these alarms it was nearly mid-day so we missed our meal, and got rations sent up to us. On this alarm we were last to return to our barracks, went to the cookhouse and I drew the ration for about twenty of us. I got all the meals out and put mine in the hot box, for I was serving, and having done so I went to get my plate of food and found it gone. Lo and behold, a L/Cpl. Harris, a real old sweat, was pouching into mine - he *hadn't* been on the exercise. I went up to him and asked him where he got the meal; he informed me that he'd got it from the hot box and what was it to do with me? I told him in no uncertain terms and threatened to punch him on the nose. At this he shouted 'Fall in two men and take Troup to the Guard Room'. I nearly had a fit, but I was saved for the alarm went again and away we went for another two days.

When we got back I thought 'bloody hell, I'm for it now'. So did Harris, but he had forgotten about our Sergeant Major who was no friend of his. He asked all about the alleged charge, I told him my version and Harris told his. The Sergeant Major told Harris that he had no reason to take my meal, he hadn't been on the alarm and had already had a meal for the day when we returned, and to cap the lot he told him that he should have renewed the charge daily which he hadn't done. Harris was very crestfallen at this and he was told to stay behind and I was told to 'bugger off' which I did with alacrity. I don't know what Harris was told but I never had a word said to me about the matter ever again from him.

Just after the episode with Harris, we were woken up one morning by an almighty bang, the electric wiring in our room caught alight and then there was a great rumble, we thought that Franco was firing at us from Algeciras over the bay. We all got up in a hurry, then there was another big bang and the chimney across from our block fell down. It wasn't any gun or shell that had done this but lightning. Several huge granite blocks of which our barracks was made had fallen over the cliff; this was what had caused the rumble. No one was hurt and we all had a laugh.

Buena Vista barracks, Gibraltar

In fact our block was at the top of a two-hundred-foot high cliff, and from the end windows we could look right down to the sea. It is a prominent spot which can be seen on any photo of the Rock looking from Africa which was about twelve miles across the Straits of Gibraltar.

Being in the band did not excuse us from Government House Guards. I did about three of these out of a possible fifteen. Once a week we did Ceremonial Guard Mounting at North Front Gates, exactly the same as takes place at the Tower of London (and just as smart). Thousands came to see us marching and counter-marching, for Gibraltar is a real tourist spot; we were cheered to the echo. When we marched through Gibraltar High Street, or Main Street as it is called, all the girls we knew came out and cheered, or booed, for it was there that we spent our nights till about 11 p.m., and got sloshed on coffee and rum at only 3d. per tot.

In each bar or cafe on the Rock was a stage and the girls did turns there, either singing or dancing. The best were the Spanish, but there were also Hungarians, Moors, French and Italians amongst them. After each turn they would come and sit with us, chatting, and the funny thing was that none of us ever made liaisons with them; all they got from us was either food or drink.

One night the girls were doing what we were told was an Adagio

31

Dancer at the Trocadero

dance, all in black veils. They really got into it, but it was boring to us and there were a few cat-calls. They got so wild that one of them in her anger fell off the stage cocking her legs right up in the air, much to the delight of us at the nearby table. Well the girl got up, I believe she was Hungarian, and she shouted at me and got our drinks and knocked them all on the floor. As a result we were kicked out of the café, naturally half cut! Anyway we got back to our beds alright and nothing further took place and when we returned the following night it had all been forgotten.

Now to speak of the Rock one must always remember that it was a sailors' town. There were only two battalions of troops there, the West Yorks Light Infantry and us, and of course the Royal Corps of Signals and the Royal Artillery, say some four thousand men, but when the Navy was in, especially with the Atlantic and Mediterranian Fleets combined, it was blue murder. I'm sure they must have vied with each other who could get drunk first, but there never was any trouble with the army and the navy, they were Matelots and we were Pongos and we drank, laughed and sang together some of the most filthy songs that can ever be heard, but no one bothered.

One night I saw the most comical sight. Usually the sailors went back by taxi. Well this night, outside one of the bars, the Trocardero I think it was, a taxi had been called and the sailors began to get in. They piled in, and in, and suddenly there was a yell and it drove off leaving a heap of fifteen or more men all piled up on top of one another. They'd gone right through the taxi and out the other door! The Naval Patrols soon sorted them out and away they went; it was never more than half a mile to any ship that was in port.

Ships in port while I was on the Rock included *H.M.S. Hood, Ramillies, Norfolk, Royal Oak, Renown, Nelson, Repulse,* aircraft carriers *Eagle, Victorious,* and *Illustrious* and numerous destroyers whose names I never knew. We also had an American destroyer, *U.S.S. Raleigh,* a four-funneller. It was a heap, and dirty, and its sailors were really untidy

Submarines and....

...destroyers in
the Naval Docks
Gibraltar
(Pictures taken
without permission)

compared to ours; they were a mixed crew as well, with some blacks on board, a thing which we had never seen on our ships. On 11th November 1937 at the American War Memorial, the Yanks were on one side and our Army and Navy on the other. When the Americans came to attention one dropped his rifle, then the same man, given the order to shoulder arms, not only dropped his bayonet but put his rifle to the wrong shoulder. I think he must have been looking at our men and not paying attention, for we slope arms with the rifle on the left shoulder while they have theirs on the right.

When the American ship was in port, there were always fights with our sailors and usually our men, being in the majority, got the better of the Yanks. We didn't like them and I suppose never will, they were so bombastic.

One day we heard some dull explosions from across the bay, two in all, and a pall of smoke began to rise from Algeciras; we saw a plane disappear in the direction of La Linea, the frontier town to Gibraltar, and that night on the radio from the B.B.C. we heard that there had been a severe aerial bombardment across the water from us. I suppose later, in 1940, Londoners would have been pleased to have had only two bombs dropped on them. Little did we know then what was in store for us.

Besides normal fatigue duties we also had to help with the married quarters, both other ranks and officers. Two things were very necessary on the Rock, cleanliness and conservation of water. There are no wells on the Rock, so water is at a premium; the only fresh water we used was for drinking purposes. We washed in salt water and everything, including kitchen utensils, was cleaned in salt water. The drains had to be flushed out at least once a month with fire hoses and we got many a laugh on this job, one in particular I shall never forget.

Our C.O. at the time was Col. Campbell; he was a real good sort and we saw little of him. To a soldier this was grand; we knew he was there and that was it. Anyway, one day my friend Pte. G. Baker, (normally known as Charlie) and I were sent to Col. Campbell's house to do the drains. This meant we had to take a large fire hose and stand. Besides this we also had to make their garden tidy, this we did and got a real nice break with a drink from Mrs Campbell, she was as pretty as a picture and it was rumoured that she was an actress. I don't doubt it at all and she was as nice as she was pretty, but we upset her without meaning to, and were never allowed to do her drains any more. It happened like this. We were told that the drain from the toilet was blocked, so I went and got the stand pipe, coupled the hose up, pulled up the drain cover and put the huge nozzle into the pipe, the trouble was that I put it into the drain to the house instead of away from the house, then I told Charlie to put the hose on full pelt and 'we'll soon clear this bloody lot'. He did, but instead of rushing away, the water went into the house and the lavatory pan and up into the air. Unfortunately, Mrs Campbell was seated on the toilet at the time. She gave an almighty yell and came running out of the house drenched from head to foot, we'd heard that stage people could swear - well she certainly did! Our ancestry suffered I can tell you, but later on, when we had got things cleared up and wiped up the mess in the house, she did have a bit of a laugh over it. We never did fatigues there any more.

34

The other job we had to do was to make sure that there were no rats near our barracks; the traps were set each night and lumps of fish were put in the traps which caught the rats alive. The place was over-run with the rats and each day at about 7 a.m. we collected the traps which usually had three or four inside, which we left outside the mess hall. How those rats suffered! Some bright sparks poured scalding hot tea over them, which took the fur completely from their bodies. It was only when the Orderly Officer made his appearance that it stopped and we handed the vermin over to a Gibraltarian who took them away and disposed of them. They were huge and really made one shudder to see them and their great fangs.

When we did duty at the frontier gate we had a Spanish 'soldier' (one of Franco's lot) at the other side of the gate to us, a big fat greasy blighter, he used to prop his rifle against the steel fence then lean on the fence and smoke a really smelly cigar, we had no conversation with him and really despised him. He treated the people from La Linea, the Spanish town near to the gate half a mile or so away, really terribly. They came to the gate for food and the Gibraltarians weren't averse to making a profit from their suffering. All the swill from the various units was brought to the frontier fence and these poor Spaniards came to get what they could scavenge from the drums the swill was brought in. Everything was in these drums, old meat, tea leaves, bread, anything that was left over from our dining halls. The people plunged their arms into the swill, but not before they had paid a penny for the privilege. They got a handful of solids and then licked their arms, eating what had stuck there. It was pitiful to see, but the Gibraltarians didn't mind, they were making a fat profit from the suffering of those poor people. We saw this, but we didn't lose any sleep over it. It was nothing to some of the suffering we were to see before long.

While at Gibraltar we were allowed to wear our civilian clothes but there was a snag - you had to have a pass and to stay out till midnight we had to have another pass. I had what was known as a P.P. or Permanent Pass, but no plain clothes pass, I went out in my uniform, 'blue patrols' which were the same as my khaki uniform only blue and a black side hat with the Britannia Badge on the side and a yellow flash to the front. I got my pass for plain clothes in the following way. Our Regiment was noted for its sports activities. We had the Army Middleweight Champion of All India, a Bandsman T.W.F. Bloxham, in

Bandsman T.W.F. Bloxham

our band and our Company Sergeant Major wanted the Company to win the Battalion Shield for boxing. He got Bloxham to train us and we became as fit as fiddles, running mile upon mile and belting hell out of the punch bag. I was classed as a Welterweight at 10st.7 lbs. and eventually came the great day when I had to fight. Well, I got a real thumping, I had won the first two rounds fighting a lad called Stone; I'd hit him with everything I'd got and hadn't turned a hair. Came the third and last round and Bloxham said "Go on, now belt him one and it's a piece of cake for you to win". I did, the only thing was he belted me harder, and I woke up with the most awful headache - he had really stoned me. Anyway I got my pass, also a point for the Company, and we won the Shield as well. Stone went on for only one more fight, for he met a naval character later on in the Rock Championships and got really hurt. It could have been me!

With the Spanish Civil War in full swing several of us had to be attached to the Navy to act as Marines on various destroyers, I was allocated with six others to *H.M.S. Vanoc*, and we were sent out daily to look for 'pirates' not Capt. Hook or Long John Silver, but ships that were supposed to be running the blockade, for at that time Britain had put sanctions on Franco's Spain, and French, German and Italian ships, especially the latter pair, were running guns to Franco and torpedoing ships as well. We were on the lookout for this type of ship or submarine; we didn't see any but it was good to be with the Navy. We lay down all day on the deck, for having studs in our boots we slipped everywhere if we stood up. It never dawned on any officer in charge to let us wear our sandals - we would have been out of uniform, wouldn't we? Some of our chaps went out on *H.M.S. Thames*, a submarine, later sunk during the war.

One fine day I was sitting on the wall at the top of the cliff near our barrack block when I saw two ships rounding Europa Point, a cruiser towing a destroyer. The latter we learned later had been torpedoed by an Italian submarine. It was never proved, but all the signs pointed to it; the torpedo had gone into the engine room, and all hands there were still inside, for to save the ship they had been sacrificed and the watertight doors sealed so they couldn't get out. The ship was brought into harbour and repaired in the dockyard, but we were not allowed to see it.

About May or June of 1938, I put in for leave and was granted an Indulgence passage to England, which cost me 7s.6d. I duly arrived at Southampton having sailed on the *Dunera* home, and found my mother in service along with my sister at Findon Park House, Findon, Sussex, near Worthing. I spent a week with them, being put up in a farm cottage on the estate, I fed the animals, being used to farm work and went to Worthing a couple of times with my mother. She was really proud of me, I was then at my present height of six feet one and a half inches, and she was five feet one inch. I went swimming and everyone used to stare at me as I was really brown. Several people asked me where I had got my tan and when I said I was a soldier on leave I was soon left alone - people didn't like servicemen in those days.

I had to return to Gibraltar eventually and sailed from Tilbury Dock on the day Chamberlain came back from Munich offering 'Peace in our Time'.

I got back to Gibraltar the day after there had been a naval battle in the Straits of Gibraltar between a Franco ship called the *Canaries* and a Government destroyer called *José Luiz Diez*. Franco's ship was sunk, and the *José Luiz Diez* had been hit just below the bridge and had a huge hole on its port side. It was anchored in mid-harbour and was being repaired although this was forbidden under some treaty and we were supposed to be neutral. It had a huge canvas cover over the hole and our people were repairing the vessel. Franco's ships were outside the harbour patrolling in the international waters, hoping to capture the ship when it left harbour. They never did, for it left during the night and we never heard of it again.

My friend Baker and I used to go for walks with another bandsman, G.A. Green. We went round the Mediterranean side of the Rock, close to the Governor's Summer Residence, we then went through

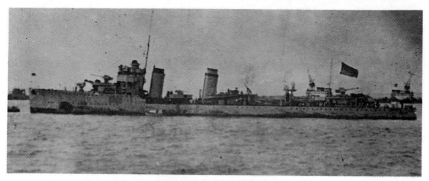

The José Luiz Diez

a cutting in the Rock and on to what was known as Windy Flats, where there were quarters for the Navy. Through there we passed the hospital and the area where the freezing plants for all the stored food on the Rock was kept. After a long walk we then went swimming and so ended our day.

I got to know a Spanish girl, about my own age, where we used to go swimming. She would come to where we were lying about and go in swimming with us, but that was as far as it got, for her mother was always with her. Apparently this is the custom. I never had time to ask her name, she was a real beauty but I never took her seriously at all. One day I had been swimming deep and I saw this body swimming over me and, thinking it was one of my friends, I struck out and hit whoever it was in the stomach. It turned out to be this young girl. What a fuss! Her mother started yelling and shouting in Spanish and waving her arms about. The girl never came swimming near me any more.

One day the German Pocket Battleship, the *Deutschland*, came into harbour; it had a huge hole in the centre of its main deck. A Spanish Government plane had dropped a bomb on to it causing considerable damage; they hadn't come to do repairs, but to bury their dead. About thirty coffins were buried, and later Hitler presented a radiogram to the base hospital for the services to the wounded. We didn't see much of the German sailors, just spoke to them while they were in Main Street, had a few drinks and appeared to get on well with them. They were not really a bad lot at all. A few days after they left, the German battleship the *Admiral Scheer*, shelled Almeria in retaliation for the hit on the *Deutschland*.

Besides hockey and football we also did some rowing - well we tried. We had competitions with the Navy and they beat us hollow. The sailors used to line the decks and jeer or cheer us, especially on the day we turned over. We were getting along fine; there were two boats, whalers, in front of us and there were about twelve of us pulling like hell, the only thing wrong was that our cox was steering us right for a buoy, instead of pulling us out of the way he shouted 'STOP!' As if we could! It was a huge thing used to tie up battleships; we hit it and over we went. Amid laughter and swearing we got on to the deck safely but didn't we rag him about the 'stop'. Pte. S. was the lad, a bandsman who was later to win the M.M. He was a real sport. In the barrack room one day he had got hold of a clock somehow, and he stated that it was unbreakable. A wag of ours named J. shouted to him 'Bring the bloody thing here and I'll show you how unbreakable it is', and he hit it with a boot and it smashed to smithereens. It was all taken in good part. J.,who left the army that year, was to become a London Fireman and died during the blitz.

Another wag we had was the C.O.'s groom - yes we still had horses, for the officers rode the animals on parades. This wag, after he had been out on the booze, used to get into a café near the barracks and sober up with a meal, but not before he always kept saying, time after time, 'Thou hast not what thou do dust, a piece of string how long' - what it meant no one knew. He also used to keep pushing Bunt Bloxham, (one of the nicest men you could wish to meet) pour tea over him, swear at him, but Bunt never turned a hair. This was what made him such a champion boxer, he kept his cool at all times.

Bloxham was sent home to England to fight in the A.B.A. Championships, where he got to the final of the middleweight division but was knocked out by a Fusilier McPhee; he was not pleased with this and blamed his defeat on his seconds and the fact that there were no Norfolks at the fight.

One day, with Bloxham and others, I was lying on the beach at North Front when a Capt. Barclay came and asked if we would do him a favour. We little knew what he was going to ask. He got us to swim out to his yacht and tie the sails up properly and batten everything down for him. It sounds simple, but in fact it was rough that day and the boat was about a quarter of a mile from the shore. Thanks to Bloxham, who was encouragement itself, I safely swam there and back, but on drying myself I got some sand in my ears and on rubbing the towel over this sand I contracted impetigo which I had for about three months. Apparently there had been oil in the water we had swum through. Capt. Barclay wasn't even there when we returned to the beach. He was the first officer to be decorated in World War Two for a raid on the Siegfried Line, winning the M.C.

Another job we had while belonging to the garrison at Gibraltar was to unload ships. We unloaded ammo. and boxed food and it was while doing this I found out how contractors swindle the army. All boxes had to be weighed and those under or over weight were opened. One such lot was extra heavy so off it came from the scales and we opened it up. It contained salmon and one tin had its paper wrapping loose so I tore it off, and under the wrapper that our people had put on in England was another one all in Chinese or Japanese writing. The same happened with a box of margarine and this stuff tasted like axle grease - it was horrible.

As with most services there was a lot of messing about and if we were on guard at Government House, and the Navy was in, if you stood at ease you could guarantee that some wag would stick an apple or an orange on your bayonet. Charlie Baker, who incidently is still alive, was a real card, he could scrounge anything, electric light bulbs, brooms, scrubbers, dustbins, we lost ours now and again, someone being short had borrowed ours, but we always managed to have the correct utensils on a Saturday morning at Company Room Inspection, Charlie had seen to that.

At one time Ivy Benson and her band visited the Rock and some of our instrumentalists got a job with her for a night; she was playing at one of the cafés there and doing a great job. To cut a long story short, some nosey parker reported Charlie, who was a cornet and trumpet player. Our B.M. went barmy; he couldn't understand why they had gone to help out a civilian orchestra without his permission.

I was once detailed to report to a Spanish Orchestra that was playing at the local opera house. They were all Spanish tunes we played and when we had to repeat a piece in practice I had to get someone to translate for me. I earned myself five pounds.

Crasher Munson who had got into trouble at Petworth Park Camp in England while we were on manoeuvres, was again in trouble, this time with the B.M., for while we were rehearsing Poet and Peasant

Overture, he crashed his part out on his double B flat bass. The part should have been played double piano. Three times he played it too loud, and each time was pulled up, till eventually he had to play it on his own. In the end he did as it was written and the B.M. was dead chuffed. Then we all had to play it with the full band, and Crasher belted it out at about double forte! The B.M. had a fit and began to choke Munson off, whereupon he lifted up his bass and threw it across the band straight at the B.M. He got seven days and was put on the draft for India.

During 1938 there was great activity on the Rock to bring it on to a war footing. We all knew that a war was on the way but with the usual British 'couldn't care less' attitude we got on with it. Ammunition for the big 9.2 inch guns was brought in by the Navy and daily these guns were let off at targets which appeared to be submarines; the guns could fire some thirty-two miles we were told. There are two of these at the top of the Rock and when fired the whole Rock shook and we heard the rumble of the shells as they went overhead.

The Ack Ack defences were terrible, in fact there were hardly any, but every item of stores was being brought in ready for war. One morning some fifty or so of us were hauled out and had to report to the docks; about forty were left on the quay, but I was one of ten who went on a barge right out of the harbour and there was the Cunard Liner *Aquitania*. A seaman from the top deck shouted out to me 'Catch this and tie it up'. I thought he meant the little line he threw down, but attached to it was the thickest rope I have ever seen - it was six inches in diameter. It took three of us to hold the thing! The barge was bobbing up and down and we weren't sailors. It took us ages to get the rope tied on to the barge, we then had to unload the nets that came down from the big ship. It took us hours and didn't we get some jeers, for there appeared to be thousands of troops on board the vessel. I suppose they were on the way to Egypt.

⊰✴⊱

Chapter 4. India

All good things must come to an end, but in spite of the crisis, the Rock carried on as usual, officers at their dances at the Rock Hotel, polo for them in the afternoons while we went swimming. We still paraded near to the Almeda Gardens, got drunk and didn't care a lot about what was happening till one day I suddenly found I was to be cross-posted to the First Battalion of The Royal Norfolk Regiment who at that time were in Delhi in India. There were about six bandsmen to go and about one hundred men from the line companies; we sailed on 24th December 1938. We could have had Christmas on the Rock, we thought, but no, we sailed on the *Dorsetshire*, another sardine can, we men below and the officers and nurses on the top deck. The voyage through the Med. was uneventful, and the sea was calm; I made certain I wasn't mess orderly and had a life of ease.

Our ship stopped at Port Said, and we all got off for a route march. We just ambled along and were met by numerous Egyptians trying to sell us goods, from useless mats to ornaments of the pyramids. Because he couldn't sell anything to our group, one of these 'gentlemen' shouted at us and an Egyptian Military Policeman gave this man a real thrashing with a long bamboo stave. He hit him unmercifully, but he didn't take much notice, running off yelling and calling back some filth or other.

Having got back on the ship we sailed again in the evening and just before nightfall we passed a large Italian troopship coming the other way on our starboard side. They waved at us and yelled and we called back asking where they had left their ice-cream barrows, then we were all cleared off deck and passed peacefully along.

Getting into the Red Sea we ran into a storm. The Bay of Biscay had nothing on this storm. We were cleared off deck and battened down; the ship rolled and twisted and went down by the prow so that at times it felt as if it were going to the bottom of the sea. Several men were sea-sick and we had plenty of food on our mess deck for a couple of days or more. We passed Aden but did not stop, so that about a week later we sighted Karachi, but even prior to seeing the coast of India an awful smell came over the whole ship. I learned later that it was the smell of the way the Indians fed their fields, all the toilets being emptied on to them. Then there was the smell of the 'hubbly bubbs'. A cake of tobacco is put on red hot charcoal and smoked through a long flexible pipe filtered through water. We really did smell India long before we caught sight of it.

Smoking a 'Hubbly bubb'

From Karachi we entrained into the most primitive carriages that could ever be imagined, just slatted seats and everything piled into where we sat, slept and ate. We must have wandered over half the continent of India, for we went first to Peshawar, then to Amritsar, Ambala and Lahore, then to Delhi. We were certainly glad to get off that train.

The 1st Battalion was at Nicholson Lines, Delhi Cantonment, some five or six miles from Delhi itself. The Battalion was split in two, the major part being at the cantonment, while the rest were at Delhi Fort in the Old City.

Travelling on the train to our destination at Delhi, we passed through mile upon mile of scrub and sandy land with small trees dotted here and there (miadam). We saw a few huts (they cannot be called houses) which appeared to be made of straw and some dark brown composition, this latter we learned was cow dung. The natives we passed seemed to be always dressed in white, not trousers like we wore, but cloth which seemed just to be wrapped round them. Of the women we saw little, but there were numerous naked children running around, and white cattle with great big horns roaming about. The huts were few and far between; we saw little of the towns we passed through but we certainly smelled them.

Upon arrival we got on an old dilapidated bus and were taken to our respective units within the Battalion. I found myself in a long bungalow made of brick and was shown to a bedcot, one of sixty or more in the one long room. I met several of the men I had been with at Aldershot and Gibraltar. Although we met old friends, it seemed very lonely to me at the time. I think I felt a little homesick, not for any home I had, but for the chums I had left behind.

In tropical kit, 1939 aged 21

The day we arrived we were introduced to curry. I hated the smell there and then, and have never to this day got used to it, but most of the men loved it. The next day we were given the usual 'short arm' inspection, then further inoculations and we were also issued with our tropical kit. At Gibraltar we had worn semi-tropical kit, but at Delhi we got the lot. Our topees were changed from the cork, high-pointed ones to pith helmets which, although larger, were much lighter. We were also issued with a belt and two pouches of leather, these to hold fifteen rounds of .303 each.

Having been issued with our kit, we had to go before the Bandmaster, who was, I learned later, a real martinet. While talking to us he could write with both hands at the same time, a feat which to me is a miracle. I was issued with a trombone and told to get to band practice straight away. There was no welcome, just 'Get on with it'.

We went through the same humdrum practising but with a difference. Usually it was marching practice and we had to be exceptionally good, for we had to attend Guard Mounting at the Viceroy's Palace. Besides marching up and down we played various items from the opera etc. Our uniform was completely white, the helmet we had was of the old type with a yellow puggaree and a yellow and black flash on the left. The topee was more or less similar to what the Royal Marines wear, but ours had a spike on top with the yellow puggaree.

The B.M. was a Mr M. Howard L.R.A.M.,A.R.C.M., and would tolerate no backsliding. He bullied everyone; even the Band Sergeant. lived in terror of him and anyone playing a wrong note got three or four hours extra practice. How we hated him.

Ceremonial Guard Mounting at the Viceroy's Palace was every week and every other day we practised marching and counter-marching till we had worn lines on the square, this being of hard baked mud. We also practised marching in a figure of eight, and when we did this in public there was usually a great cheer.

Guard duty at the Viceroy's Palace

We had our instruments inspected every week. We had them spotless inside and out, but one day, coming back from the palace, I let my trombone hit the edge of the lorry we were travelling in, the slide stuck and next day was instrument inspection. There was nothing to do but go into the native village and get the 'mistree' (the local handyman) to beat it out. How he did it I do not know, but he did and my instrument passed inspection - lucky for me.

The barracks in the cantonment covered about a square mile, inside which we had a church and a huge canteen run by an Indian named Khada Bux. We could usually get anything there at night, for during the day we had the 'char wallahs' coming round. We got a mug of tea, a wad (cake), or apples, oranges or mangoes. We had to see that the skin of this fruit, including bananas, was not broken as this could have caused us to get enteric or some other fever, for India has numerous diseases unheard of in this country and it was certainly no good chancing it.

45

The char wallah had numerous names in his book, for we could get what he had to sell on tick and you might be told by him that he wanted to see Tommy Tucker, John Wayne, Humphrey Bogart, and Errol Flynn, who owed him money. It only cost about five annas for a tea and wad, but still we booked up.

We used to get a good laugh when the char wallah was collecting his debts, for invariably he was called a 'thieving bastard' and he used to say, 'Why call me thieving bastard on Monday, Tuesday and Wednesday, when on the other days you call me Robin Redbreast?' There was no answer to that. He did a good trade and we could get any of his wares from about 9 a.m. till 7 p.m. when he disappeared. He was a Sikh and had been with our Regiment for years.

All the blocks except the band block were of two storeys, about ten blocks in double lines and in between were the usual services which go with a regiment. The orderly room, plus the administration block and medical services were all contained in this area and far out, right away from everyone else, was the guard room and the cells. I knew before long that the guard room was a long way from our block through the following taking place: we had been called out to a riot in Delhi about 7 a.m., resulting in us having to be in the city centre near the main Hindu Temples. There were also several Muslims and Sikhs in the area and they were all having a real good go at each other when we arrived. There were some from Delhi Fort and our lot from the cantonment. We had all been issued with twenty rounds of .303 ammo., so we were told to kneel down and, on the order, fire a volley over the natives' heads, but as soon as we knelt down, the whole lot disappeared like leaves in autumn. We remained in the area for some hour or more, but there was no more trouble so we all returned to barracks. In any case I wouldn't have fired for I intended not to dirty my rifle.

Well on return to barracks, (it was my 21st birthday, on the 21st March 1939 that this incident took place), I got back into our block, took the bolt out of my rifle and went to hand it over with my ammo, but lo and behold I saw that I only had fifteen rounds - five had disappeared! I looked and looked and the key orderly refused to take either rifle or ammo in. He told Cpl. Lord, our room N.C.O., what had taken place and Lord informed me that unless I found the ammo by 9 a.m. I would be on a charge for losing it. I said 'Yeah' and he said 'Yeah, for insolence to an N.C.O.' Anyway, after much sweat, I found the ammo; it had

Scene of the riot in Delhi

fallen into my kitbox so I was O.K. as far as that was concerned, for it was an acknowledged fact that it was one month in Lucknow Detention Barracks for every round lost. At 9 a.m. I was on Company Orders and appeared before Capt.Trixie Cubitt. Every time I began to speak to defend myself he shouted 'Shut up!', so I did and received seven days for insolence.

The Provost Sergeant was called Rat Hiley. He was real mean and as soon as I reported for Jankers he laughed and rubbed his hands saying, 'At last I've got one of those bloody bandsmen'. The first day I got the cells to scrub out, and as soon as I stopped for a minute's blow he was behind me, telling me that if I stopped again I would occupy a cell. Then another day I had to whitewash the stones all along about a mile of roadway. I got through my seven days eventually and kept my nose clean for the rest of my service with Lord, but I got my own back good and proper.

'A' Company was that part of the battalion stationed at Delhi Fort; they did the Viceroy's Guard and were known as the 'Foreign Legion'. They would put a Regiment of Guards to shame, in fact our Regiment was called the 'Guards of the East'. Discipline was very strict in every way, pack drill in the heat of the afternoon for the most minute of drill offences and it was two weeks pack drill for anyone who caught V.D. There were some who did, but not many. Our tour of duty abroad was for six years. Gibraltar was counted as a Home Station as was Malta, Egypt being the first station abroad. It was no good getting browned off and no man was allowed to be without money. Over the years several men in various units had committed suicide by shooting themselves, but in our unit sport was encouraged in every way, our C.O. at the time being a Col.Thorne from Heacham, Norfolk. Everything was done to keep up morale; some fifty or so were even allowed to marry native girls.

With Charlie Baker I did a lot of running. We would start about

4 p.m. and run till 6 p.m., have our dinner (the main meal of the day was in the evening), then afterwards we would play football then go up the canteen for 'crummy steak' (liver with bread crumbs), or 'undi banjo' (eggs and bread), or there was the usual steak with roast potatoes and tomatoes. We lived well and it usually cost about two rupees for the lot, no matter what we had.

Some days we ran so long and far that we did not bother to come in for our meal. One day we were earlier than usual and I saw a hare running across our path. I bent down, picked up a stone and threw it, hitting the animal right between the eyes; we had it for dinner, stewed. One day I was all on my own running and I met a huge Sikh. I am 6'1½" tall and he made me look small. He ran beside me in all his robes and began to chat, but I ran towards the barracks and lost him. At that time Sikhs were rioting in Lahore and Amritsar, and those cities were not far away.

The area of the cantonment was very flat, and it didn't take much out of Charlie Baker and I to run, but it could be dangerous too. The whole area was covered in scrub and small trees, and now and again we came across isolated villages, but we steered clear of them. One day in the hot weather we passed near to one of these villages. We came across some small idols, about six inches tall, at the corner of a dried-up field. Instead of leaving well alone we kicked these over without thinking, and suddenly there were about fifty natives chasing us, yelling at the top of their voices. I suppose they had been put there to worship during the day while they were working. No wonder the Hindus hated us.

Another time we ran along the Jumna River, and we could see a great big fire, with a crowd around it. Naturally we had to look, and from about two hundred yards we saw a person or body suddenly sit up in the middle of the flames and one of the persons looking on picked up a great big lump of wood and hit whoever the corpse was upon the head and the whole body disintegrated. Didn't we run! This was a ritual funeral and we weren't going to get mixed up in any row.

Another time, whilst running along the great trunk road into Delhi, we saw a great big car by the side of the road. There was no one about and it had curtains round the windows and darkened glass at the front. Charlie opened the car door and wasn't there a yell! There were women inside and they were Hindus; being in Purdah, no man other than their husbands should have seen them and we had made them unholy.

Run? We ran like hell and did not stop till we got back to our lines.

With all our equipment I suppose you might wonder how we ever got time to play. Well it was easy, for with our pay of about ten rupees per week we lived like lords. We wore drill shirt, vest, shorts and trousers and each day bar Sunday our drill was collected and washed. This cost us eight annas per week, about tenpence. Then we had all our equipment cleaned and polished including our bayonets, boots, topees and leather belts, plus having our beds made up and swept out for another eight annas per week. We were also provided with a mug of tea each morning for this princely sum. The only thing not cleaned by our bearers was our rifles - they were sacred.

Each bearer or servant cleaned up about ten men and when he woke us in the morning he always greeted us with 'salaam Sahib'; we also got shaved in bed. Besides making up our bedcots the bearers also had to take down our mosquito nets. What a life! It was no wonder some of the chaps had been out in India for twelve years or more.

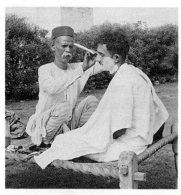

Shaving

Our beds were exactly the same as we had in England except that they didn't push in half, but every Thursday we had to 'bug out'. The place was alive with bugs, millions of them; we burnt them out with a blow-lamp. It was not practicable to dodge this chore for the bugs bred like wildfire and the N.C.O. in charge had to sign that we had all done this. We had to move our beds out on to the veranda and do the job there, but when the job was done we had the rest of the day off.

By March or April the heat had got to about 120 degrees in the shade and there *was* no shade. Our faces, knees and hands got really brown, and we certainly didn't sunbathe. It was rumoured that our bungalow had got mixed up with a design that had to be built in England; it was like a hot-house. Although there was a window it was kept shut. Overhead was a punka; this wafted to and fro, but now and again the electricity broke down and it had to be worked by 'outside labour'. An Indian pulled a rope so that the punka kept moving the hot air about. Now and again you would feel the room getting hotter and hotter - the man working the punka had gone to sleep! Someone would throw a bucket of water over him and he would pull after that, at least until he went to sleep again. No wonder they loved us!

During the very hot weather the doors were opened and Kus Kus Tatties filled the space, these tatties were large moss and reed breaks, water was thrown on them and the wind did the rest, cooling the air down in the room. On Orders there were always warnings about 'heavy hogging' in the afternoons. We didn't work; some like Charlie Baker and I ran about and were called 'nuts' for it, but it kept us fit and gave us something to do, which was the main idea.

Each night there was always a beer up, we used to take it in turns, three or four of us would buy a sack of beer, about forty bottles; we drank this easily and the sweat would run out of us. You may have heard of drinking oneself sober - we did just that.

After the heat on the plains of Delhi got to average between 110 and 120 degrees, the Battalion went to a hill station in the lower Himalayas. First we went by train to Dehra Dhun, then about forty miles march each day till we got to Chacrata. Marching up the hills was a real bind. We stopped at a place called Sia Rest Camp en route, stayed the night, fed and off we went crossing the river at Kalsi River Bridge. The river was dried up, but it was some half-mile across; during the rainy season it must have been a real hazard for there were huge boulders everywhere. I was glad there was a bridge.

A brief rest on the march from Dehra Dhun

The road up the hills was very narrow, about twelve feet wide. It was divided into 'gates' so that movement on them was so many hours for up traffic and so many for down. Our camp or barracks was some eighteen thousand feet up and it took us all our time to march and breathe. There was no singing or whistling (as you see in certain films) I can tell you. After three days we got to our destination and then we had three days for recovery and acclimatisation - we needed it.

All the heavy equipment was brought by lorry, but the unloading job was done by the hill people of the area; they could carry three hundredweights on their backs with ease. They would tie the load up and attach it to a band which went round their heads. It looked impossible for any human being to carry so much. They could carry at least ten kitbags each and think nothing of it. They got ten annas per load, paid on the spot.

The hills were steep; looking over the sides you could see a drop of thousands of feet. Some were covered by brush and large trees and in these trees were monkeys which had white fur round their faces; they never came near but kept twittering in the trees and giving the most outlandish yells. This carried on till late at night.

There was no parade ground as such. From each bungalow it was direct into the jungle, for that was what it was. All doors were locked at night in case we had a 'loose Wallah' visit us. These were thieves and often one was caught or shot attempting to steal a rifle, but nothing took place like that while we were up the hills. They were hard to catch, for they would grease themselves all over with cheetah fat. Dogs were afraid of the smell, and once caught they could not be held because of the fat on their arms.

Band practice was the order of the day, and we gave several concerts. We did not have to use our mosquito nets which was a blessing. Our dress was the same, except that we wore a pullover. It may have been about 80 degrees, but after 120 degrees on the plains it felt very cold, especially at night.

We went down from our hill station by bus. It frightened the life out of me. We had native drivers, the kit was in the middle of the bus and we could hardly move. Luckily there were no windows in the vehicle and with the twisting and turning and nearly going over the edge, several men were sick all over their equipment.

When we got to Dehra Dun we were due for breakfast. We were

given the old army standby of boiled eggs, but the way the eggs were boiled is unbelievable. They were put into dixies (cooking buckets) and then put under the brake steam pipe of the engine which was to pull the train. Steam was then shot into the dixies, this lasted about ten minutes for each batch. Well, we all got three eggs each. Boiled? They weren't quarter boiled, all but raw they were, and then it started. Someone threw an egg on to the track, being unable to eat it or even drink it, and then

another went the same way, but instead of going on to the track it hit the carriage. Then, as if ordered, everyone threw their eggs at the train, it was running yellow! The senior officers were doing their nuts. You really could not blame the men, it was the Cook Sergeant's fault for believing that the steam could have cooked the eggs for some eight hundred men.

Steam locomotive of the N.W. R.

Back at Delhi we got into the usual routine again, Guard Mounting and band practice with occasional Officers Mess duties. While they bawled their heads off, having imbibed well, we played all the usual musical hits; ' Smoke Gets In Your Eyes' was the then top of the pops for them, it was years old but they loved it.

One thing that got me down was our toilets, they were the dry type, they were away from the main bulding and if visited at night you had to take a torch, but during the day there was always a native in charge of them, and he used to take a delight in nearly castrating us and I am sure he kept watch beneath, for as soon as you got finished the bucket was whipped away and now and again you would see the native running and a soldier chasing him, having nearly had an injury done to him. The toilets were collected each day round about noon, a bullock with a big container took the lot away; we called it the Bombay Mail.

The worst thing that could happen to you when out in semi-jungle near the cantonment was to be caught in a sand-storm. You would see a dirty big black cloud on the horizon, then a cold wind and then it was upon you. If out, it was best to lie down, but if in the bungalows we used to batten down; all doors and windows were shut and we sat there and waited for it to pass, usually in about half an hour. Sand was everywhere, under and in beds, boots, equipment, eyes, mouth and ears and the floor had about a half inch of it. The bearers had a real job getting us clean again.

Following the sandstorms came the monsoons. If you've seen rain, you can never believe what a monsoon is like. We had monsoon ditches everywhere, about eight feet wide and six feet deep, and when the rain came, it just dropped down, the drains would be full up in about five minutes and roaring away. We had one man drowned in one. If caught in the open, you could hardly see - it came down in rods.

All around was the semi-jungle or 'miadam'. This was criss-crossed with 'nullahs' or deep crevices; you steered clear of them for there were hyenas in them, and jackals and dead dogs. One had to be especially careful for these animals could give you rabies. I came across a half dead jackal one day with Charlie, it kept trying to get up to attack us so we killed it with a boulder and put it out of its misery, but that day I came back and inside the band practice room there was, as I thought, a great big dog ferociously eating some meat and a bone. Some of the lads were careless how they left their dogs with food. This thing sprang at me and I just had time to close the door and yell for the Regimental Dog Shooter. He disposed of it, but it was not a dog - it was a dirty great jackal.

Now each regiment had a dog shooter; he was a sniper, and any dog running loose, day or night, was shot by him no matter whose dog it was, the C.O.'s or anyone's. One day we were on parade and a dog ran right across our front, it was the B.M.'s and bang! it was dead. The shooter then cut off its tail and got a native to see that the body was burned; the tail got him another round of ammo. 12 bore for the one he had used. That was how my dog ended up and I could not say a word. It was my fault and that was that. I didn't keep any more dogs in India.

It was in Delhi that we learned we were at war with Germany. We knew it was coming, but were told we wouldn't move; we were wanted to guard the Viceroy's Palace. Some pipe dream that was! It was at 5 p.m. on a Sunday night that we heard Prime Minister Chamberlain announce the news, and you will laugh, for I sat there and thought 'How the bloody hell are we going to march back all that way?'. I just hadn't a clue what war really meant.

Prior to leaving Delhi we had the usual and unusual round of parades. We saw Sikhs in all their finery; these were tall men, bearded and wearing long red tunics fringed with gold; they had red turbans and long lances, this was how they stood guard. They had baggy white trousers, baggier than most natives, for it was said that the Son of God would somehow come from a Sikh, and that the baggy trousers were so that the baby God would not drop on the floor.

The Sikhs had been the most loyal of all the native troops during the Indian Mutiny; they were respected for what they were, a real fine body of men. The other native soldiers, or Sepoys, envied them. Later they all proved their loyalty to the British Raj as it was called and fought all over the world with distinction.

Soldiers of the Viceroy's Guard

Chapter 5. Bangalore

Eventually we were told we were to move, but it was not until we were at the Cantonment rail station that we found that we were going to Bangalore in Southern India.

Getting to Delhi main station an incident took place which cost one of our lads seven days jankers. The porters could carry anything they were loaded up with like camels. Well this porter came up, was loaded up with the kit of the man who had engaged him and put it on the train. But instead of paying him, our man refused and wrote on his coat. Each porter had a blue coat and on the left breast in English were the following words which I shall never forget:– 'One Anna Per Person Per Trip' - 1½d. for carrying a huge load. Imagine a porter in England accepting that amount! But to add insult to injury our wag wrote underneath 'Perhaps', and just at that precise moment our Company Officer arrived. Not only was the man paid, but our lad had to pay the man double and got seven days on the spot. All these little things added up and made the natives dislike us, to say the least.

We had the usual carriages, except that this time there were windows in the compartments. We had all our equipment plus all the pets you can imagine, parrots, monkeys, and last of all dogs; these were the worst. We were on road for five days and five nights and must have wandered all over India in that time. Troop trains apparently just move on lines that are free for little periods and make innumerable stops. When we did stop it was usually with jungle all round and we did not go into that for fear of snakes and leeches. I think our average speed must have been 20 – 30 m.p.h. and at times, to get a little exercise, we jumped off and ran alongside. We passed through Ghandi's birthplace without stopping. Eventually we came to Madras and after the engines had been changed and one put on the back with two up front, we started the uphill climb to Bangalore where we arrived early one morning.

We marched from the station through about a mile of native huts or houses made of straw mixed with cow dung, the sheep, goats and cattle being in the dwelling with the occupants; they had fires inside as well.

Bangalore proper we found to be just like a European village or small town; the buildings were almost the same and the bungalows had great sweeping lawns and front gates like anywhere in England.

On our arrival at our quarters we found it was called Baird Barracks; it was walled all round, and in front of the main gate was a huge grass area where every day we saw a cricket match in progress. We used it also as our sports ground.

Over the cricket field was Bangalore proper, where there were bars with English names like the 'Bull and Bush' and in each were numerous Eurasian girls. You could dance with them if you wanted. I didn't, not because I didn't want to but because I cannot dance. These bars were always full up.

I did go to a Residency dance once, but only once. There was a good-looking girl there. She refused to dance and I got stroppy, but I understood why when she stood up - she was about five foot nothing and I was 6' 1½". I never tried again.

In Bangalore 1940

With two of my friends, both bandsmen, we went all over the place visiting all the monuments and buildings of note, especially the museum where we saw a sheep with hind quarters front and rear and its head in the middle of its stomach, and petrified cats in all manner of poses.

Bangalore is in Mysore State where the temperature never got above 90 degrees. After being on the plains of Delhi it was really grand, nice and cool. We had the usual bugs, but there were also red ants to contend with. Inside the barracks were quite a lot of trees. I couldn't make out at first what the great big black things hanging from the branches were, but in the evening I soon found out that they were huge bats. They did not attack at all but flew about squawking at everything all night; we soon got used to them. We were allowed to wear civvies; trousers and jacket cost ten rupees to have made; we went to the 'dersi' or tailor in the morning to be measured and by 4 p.m. the same day we had our civvies.

Our shoes were made of the best leather possible. Again we went in the morning, got measured, and by lunch time they were made. If you wanted to you could stand there and see them done. One thing I was amazed to see was that instead of a knife the 'moochi' or bootmaker used a chisel; it was sharpened up on emery paper and slipped through the leather like greased lightning. Usually we did not stay to see our shoes and clothes made because the dersi and the moochi smoked hubbly bubbs and they stank.

In Bangalore we were always broke. We used our blue lights and each pay day had to pay on these the amount we had borrowed, each blue light being worth one rupee at the canteen. We used our other money in the city. We used the best hotels and always came back by ghari, that is a horse-drawn four-wheel or two-wheel carriage. It cost about eight annas from anywhere to our barracks gate, the last one out paying, but now and again there used to be some yelling and shouting, for instead of paying where there had been six or seven in the ghari and all being half drunk, the men used to stand there and give three cheers and run. Usually the Guard Commander stopped these men and all had to pay double for their cheek, but a lot got away with it.

Nearly all the officers that we saw were taking out white women, or some half castes. They had a really good time. Polo was the order of the day and nearly all had horses, with plenty of grooms or 'cyces' to look after the animals. It was a cushy life for them.

Things progressed easily at first, then suddenly the screws were put on and we did arms training nearly all day except for us bandsmen who did first aid (being stretcher bearers), five to a company with our own L/Cpl. We had our usual sports in the evening, football, cricket and running, and field sports.

At evening time both Charlie Baker and I used to run miles and this was the cause of my getting a real telling off. It was Battalion Sports Day and I was not entered in anything so I had got myself a load of soda pop and had drunk about five bottles. I was lying there at peace with the world when the Coy. Sgt.Major told me to report to the sports field in running kit. I demurred, but an order is an order and I had to obey. Getting to the sports field I found that one of the Company runners in the mile had called off. I was full of pop, but just had to line up. I ran at an easy lope for the first two laps and on the third I was in front. It seemed a piece of cake. I must have heard the bell for the last lap, but for some reason took no notice. About four men passed me and then I woke up, finished fifth and didn't I get a telling off! We did *not* win the Battalion Shield!

With Charlie Baker before the monument to the Maharajah of Mysore

Rumours were rife in the battalion as to what was going to happen to us. We had some Territorials come out to join us, and with them our unit was up to war strength; then the rumours began to fly. We were going to Egypt, or Malaya - we all wanted to go to Malaya, but thank God we didn't. The battalion was then split up again and off these men went. I think they landed at Singapore, just ready to be captured by the Japs, for they were put in the 4th, 5th, and 6th Norfolks who were all captured there and suffered terribly on the Burma Railway.

Training was getting to its peak in the unit and we were issued with the Bren Gun. This gun we learned was made in Czechoslovakia at the town of Brno. We learned everything we could about this weapon and could take it to pieces for cleaning blindfold; it had a 22" arc of fire, could be dropped, and the mag. held 29 rounds of .303, its stoppages were almost nil and it was easy to carry. Being the tallest in the section I usually got this job – being tall has disadvantages as well as advantages.

Cutting coconuts

Training now being under way, we marched out of Bangalore to a place called Magardi, some 24 – 25 miles away along the most sandy roads you can imagine. We halted every hour and got the natives who followed us to climb the trees and cut coconuts down for a drink, for we were forbidden to use our water bottles. We marched the first ten or so miles with a halt every hour, then we went full pelt for the next fourteen or so without a halt. Still, when we got to camp the tents were up and we flopped out, but not before the laughable call of 'Get out with your feet' rang out. Next day training began in earnest.

All the training we did was concentrated on this road to Bangalore, and all were withdrawal schemes, never once an attack. The British Army is known for its strategic withdrawals and I am certain that it was only with the influx of the conscripts and their new ideas that it altered. The best laugh we had was when we had to 'fire' at the enemy, usually at about three hundred yards; it gave our positions away right off, but that was how it was done. We did not use ammo. but had a tin full of stones with each Bren or V.B. gun (similar to the Bren and British made). This we rattled to imitate the gun firing. We had no bombs to fire, we did not even have a mortar, just a stick of bamboo some two inches in diameter and this was stuck on two legs; when it 'fired' the man in charge had to shout out 'BANG!'. What a way to run an army! The British Army had rested on its laurels a long time, but laurels don't win wars, as we were soon to find out to our cost.

Chapter 6. A Long Voyage

One day my bearer came in and told me we were going to leave Bangalore and go to the Middle East. About a week later we packed up bag and baggage and left all our kit in secured boxes, being told we would get it back one day. (I did get mine after the war - it was delivered to my home address.)

The bearers' grapevine was true, we marched off, much to the delight of the natives; literally millions came to see us off and cheered like hell. We travelled on the usual troop train, but were only on it for two days, getting to Bombay one wet and windy morning. We were ordered out of the train, collected our bottles of lime (we always had five bottles per day while on troop trains) and got under some old trucks for shelter. We then began loading up the most rotten ship you ever did see. It was a P & O boat called the *Eastern Prince*, it had previously been used to take pilgrims to Mecca, but now it had us. We loaded ammo all day till nightfall, then on board we went.

Getting on board ship was easy, living aboard was much worse. We had come out to India in peace time; it was war now and we carried about twice as many as normal. The decks were full of troops and there was hardly a place to stand never mind sling a hammock. I made sure I was not mess orderly and found a spot on the top deck where I could lay my hammock at night. The rest of my kit was bunged below decks, as was everyone else's. We had the Ulster Rifles with us to make matters worse and they were real bolshies.

When we sailed, which was in the morning, I thought of all that ammo beneath, shells, ball ammo and flares etc., if we had been hit by a torpedo we would have gone up like a mushroom.

First day out we sailed due West. The next day the ship altered course, we saw this by the wake, and we then sailed South. We thought this was funny, but it was posted on the bulletin board that Italy had declared war, so instead of going towards the Red Sea we carried on South.

After the first few hours on board we had boat drill; every man had to wear a life jacket, with a red torch on the shoulder which we had to switch on if ever we were in the water. We tested these and they were

O.K. and then we were told that the ship's siren would sound seven blasts if we had to abandon ship. We were all allocated a point on the ship's sides so that every inch of the sea could be seen at all times; we worked two hours on and four off, looking for the periscopes of submarines. Every point of the compass was manned at all times, day and night.

Eventually we got towards the coast of South Africa, some few miles from Durban, and besides doing look-out duties I was on a gun at the rear of the ship. I think it was a 3.5; there was a marine gun-layer with us but he did not even show us how to load, never mind fire the beastly thing. He was in the wet canteen all day drinking beer. However, as we approached Durban, a County Class Cruiser came up out of nowhere and tailed behind. The gun-layer did his nut and told me and Charlie Baker that we were lucky that the cruiser hadn't opened fire and sunk us. It would have been our fault if it had, he said. Well I told him in no uncertain terms where he got off. 'It's either the *London* or the *Norfolk* that ship,' I said, 'it's British and we both know it well'. What he did not know was that we had seen the County Class ships at Gibraltar and knew them as well as he did, if not better. We had no more bother with him, but he still didn't show us how to load, fire, or lay the gun.

When we got to Durban we were given two grand days ashore. We were the first British troops there since World War One, and we were invited out and shown the sights. I did one day of this and then went out with Charlie Baker. We saw natives pulling rickshaws; they wore skins and had large cow horns on their heads, and round the calves of their legs what appeared to be fur. They called us 'Baas'. We were taken to a picture house and during the performance you could eat a meal and still look at the picture on the screen (the 'Wizard of Oz'). The tune that was all the rage was 'South of the Border, down Mexico way' but the South Africans had altered this to 'South of the Border near Culliman Way'. It must have meant something to them, but not to us.

From Durban we eventually arrived at Capetown. When I awoke one morning, the ship had stopped, and from our deck I could see Table Mountain - it was a grand sight. We paraded on the docks and marched through Cape Town. During our three days there the Australians arrived on the troopship *Lancashire*; they gave us a great cheer and when we went ashore that day the city got woken up, believe me. We went to the City Hall and received an address of welcome from the Mayor and were then left on our own. We wandered all over the place; some of the lads were invited into the homes of the townspeople, others got rides to the top of Table Mountain.

At Capetown some forty or more of the Ulster Rifles deserted. We sailed without them, but if they had hoped to dodge active service they had another think coming, for after about four weeks sailing we collected them up in chains at Takoradi on the Gold Coast, along with three Norfolks who hadn't been missed. They all told of the tough time they had had with the South African Police, but no one cared a hoot - they should not have deserted.

The County Class *H.M.S. London* was our escort and we were joined by six destroyers. We were, it appeared, an important convoy consisting of the *Regine Del Pacifico*, *Orontes*, *Kenya*, and two other liners besides ourselves.

One day we suddenly found that we had no escort. This gave us a fright I can tell you, but they turned up a couple of days later just before we went into Freetown. We got off there on barges and all went for a swim. Some clot began to rock the barge we were on and it nearly went over. There was a great yell from the crew and this was stopped, for there must have been some two hundred standing men. I thought myself it was dangerous and was ready to swim for it.

For two whole weeks we sailed North West, still looking for subs. I am sure I saw one every minute of the day. Our duty had been altered then to one hour on and two off every 24 hours. One day about noon, our ship's siren went off. After four blasts we all ran to our boats. It got to seven blasts and carried on and then the whole ship went silent. The engines had stopped; the rest of the convoy was speeding ahead with the escort and there we were on a flat sea, a sitting target for any U Boat. Our boilers had broken down and had to be repaired. We lay like this for some four hours - we all stood or lay on deck at our lifeboats - it was the longest four hours I have ever spent.

Eventually we were repaired and we 'stood down', but our watch carried on with a greater earnestness than before.

Now on board ship we had no bearers; we did our own washing

and cleaning. This was fine, but we could not use fresh water and our soap did not lather in the salt water we had to use, so like most soldiers we improvised. We used our duree ropes, being part of our bedding, which we used on land to tie up our blanket and duree (mat). At sea we had hammocks, but we kept the rope and it turned out to be a godsend. We got our clothing, slacks, shirts, vests, socks etc., and tied them up and threw the line over the side for a couple of hours; the clothing was bashed against the ship and came out spotless.

One day the Regimental Sergeant Major put his washing over the side. Normally the portholes were screwed tight, but someone or other (we never found out who) opened a porthole and cut the rope. The Sergeant Major saw it done, but could do nothing. He had Company Sergeant Majors and Sergeants etc., running around like headless chickens looking for the culprit, but naturally he was never found.

About a week out from England, we ran out of fresh water and razor blades; we were allowed only our tea to drink, for the beer also ran out and the whole ship was on edge and bolshie. Also some bright sparks had been whipping the buttons off our greatcoats; these had a figure of Britannia on them and there were no Quarter Master's Stores to get replacements. All the button threads had been cut by razor blade, nice and clean, so, on finding that all my big buttons had gone, I went round with my razor blade and collected a full set, five large and seven small, and I did not sew them back on till the night before we got to Liverpool. This we knew because we sailed close to the North of Ireland, and some Ulsters recognised the landmarks.

Having passed into the Irish Sea there were a series of the most terrific bangs. We all ran to the sides of the ship and found that the destroyers were depth-charging; they dropped ten or twelve and then all was quiet. The first thing we saw of Liverpool was the Liver Bird on the top of the Liver Building, and then the whole panorama of the city came into view. Getting up to the quay, our boat passed several bombed out wrecks, but we were safe.

Looking over the side we saw a sight we had never seen before, We were still in the old army uniform, but the M.P.s there were in what was then modern battle dress. They did look a fright, but we must have looked a fright to them, for we were in buttoned khaki tunic with puttees round our legs, just like peace time. Our topees and leather equipment had been confiscated on board. The people looked at us dumbfounded.

63

And we looked at them, especially the girls - they looked wonderful - all their faces really looked beautiful and we all had wet eyes, it was so grand to have got back to England. Just prior to leaving the ship we were informed that the army had been defeated at Dunkirk. We could not believe it, but we never thought for one moment that we were going to be defeated, and we never were.

As I had been on look-out all night prior to landing, I know little or nothing of our journey south. I lost my cap badge, that's all I know, but woke up at some station or other and we were taken to Lingfield by bus. I was one of the lucky ones, who were granted an immediate five days leave. How we moaned! Five days! It wasn't enough.

On my five days I found out where my mother was. She was at a place called Wargrave in Berkshire. I called and saw her, but I could not stay with her, so off I went to London and met several of the lads who were staying at the Union Jack Club, a big army hotel. All we had to do was show our pass and pay book and we got in. I stayed a couple of days and then went to Aylsham in Norfolk to find Baker. I stayed the night with him and then next day we were told to report to Ashtead in Surrey.

Getting to Ashtead I found that H.Q. Coy. had been billeted all over the place, the band was broken up for the moment and we all got various jobs. I was made battalion meat storeman of all things, and what a job that was! As it happened it only lasted one day for me. I got into real trouble, not under military discipline but over what I did with the issue of the rations for the companies. It happened like this.

We had a whole big issue of meat delivered and put in a cold store in a shop that had been taken over. Well I cut up and dished out all the meat for dinner next day, that is the midday meal for N.C.O.s and Other Ranks, and evening meal for the Officers. This is where I came unstuck, all the companies had their meat and I was congratulated by the Messing Officer for doing a good job on my first day. I had got all the ration slips piled up and was making a list of what had been issued, but one slip had dropped on to the floor and had been trodden on over and over again so that it was unrecognisable, in fact I didn't know it was there till the Officers' Mess Cook came along and asked for their rations, some twenty-five officers or more. Rations? There weren't any; all I had was tins of bully, and then the fur began to fly! The officer went into a rage, called me all the names under the sun, but there was no fresh meat.

The result was that the Officers Mess dined out that night, and I was relieved of duty at the ration store. Bang went any chance of promotion in that area!

We had not really got into the swing of the war yet; we still had our old service dress, brass buttons and all. We did a lot of elementary training on rifle, Bren and mortar, i.e. aiming and loading, and strength holds for the rifle. We also did numerous route marches and kept fit in this way. In the evening after 5 p.m. we were free and being summer time, June or July, we went out. I don't remember Ashtead at all, but I do remember Epsom which was small and snobbish. What they were snobbish about beats me, for apart from the racecourse it had not much to offer. One night Charlie, Dodger and myself went out for a walk. We saw a café and went in for a cup of tea, but we were politely shown the door and the *notice*. It said 'DOGS and SOLDIERS NOT ALLOWED'. I will never forget that notice - had we been invaded they would have sung a different tune!

One thing took place which was, so it was alleged, a disgrace to our unit. A pub got bombed during one of many air raids in the area and the guard on our battalion HQ turned out and helped to find the people who had been wounded or buried under the rubble. They did all this but our lads then got stuck into the drink that was lying about, and were found drunk when it came to be relieved. The Guard Commander and his guard of six were immediately arrested, court martialled and got various sentences from six to nine months, the N.C.O. losing his stripes as well. It was all in the papers, and we were told that Churchill had given instructions for the men to be made an example of. They had been charged with looting besides being drunk. It didn't go down too well, but technically speaking they were guilty of the offences as charged.

One the other hand we had several Canadians in our area, all soldiers, and they were boisterous to say the least. They were always being arrested by our M.P.s for drunkenness, but Churchill came down on the side of the Canadians, stating that they were only boisterous colonials and we should expect this type of behaviour. I was glad when I left Ashtead to go as an orderly to the 20th Guards Brigade H.Q. at Pyrford Hall, Woking, Surrey, along with Charlie and one other man.

It was an easy life at the H.Q. The Brigadier was a Fox-Pitt, the Brigade Major was Lord Ross, the Intelligence Officer was a Major Head and the Staff Captain was Capt. Heber Percy of the Grenadier Guards. All of them came from some Guards Regiment or other, but believe me I was the tallest there. The Welsh appeared to be no taller than the men in our own unit and the others were about equal to myself. They were all young soldiers.

One day we had a visit from H.M. the King, and we all paraded outside the hall on a terrace there. It was pointed out that we had recently arrived from the East and we all three stood there together; the King did not take a scrap of notice, just passed us by as if we were something the cat had left behind. We did not think much of that.

In the grounds of the hall was a wide and deep stream, it was suggested that we should all go for a swim. We did. Mine lasted about two seconds flat! I dived in and nearly died of fright; it may have been hot weather, but to us it was freezing cold. I could not get out quick enough. Never again did I go for a swim in the open air, not till we eventually got abroad again.

We did drill with the guardsmen and were just as good as them although they had different words of command. We were told to 'fall in', but they had a call 'get on parade'. This call to us meant to get out of the room or barracks and on to the parade ground. To them it meant to 'fall in'. We did not know this, so one day Charlie and I stood waiting to fall in when the Drill Sgt., an enormous soldier called Flynn, bawled out 'Get on parade!' We stood where we were. We saw the others moving forward and lining up, but we stood still. Flynn bawled out, 'You dozey men there, get on parade!. Both of us turned round and I said 'Who's the daft bugger he's yelling at?' Well it was us, and didn't Flynn lace into us. We got three days extra drill for it, done at double time. We 'got on parade' double quick after that.

The next thing that made me laugh and proved that these guardsman were still infants in the army was that one of them came up and started asking me something and began with 'Corporal'. I took no notice, not being a corporal, and he kept this up till at last I realised he was talking to me. I laughed and said 'I'm not a bloody Corporal, I'm like you, a Private or Bandsman if you like, but don't call me Corporal'. He then asked what the two stripes on my left arm were for, I told him they were for five years good conduct or undetected crime. He laughed

66

and I went on to explain to him how our unit worked and that one stripe on the upper arm was a Lance Corporal and two stripes was a full Corporal they did not have these ranks in the regiment he was in. L/Cpls. all had two stripes and after that three for Sergeants as we did.

I worked in the Orderly Room at Brigade H.Q. taking signals over for transmission to St.John's Wood in London. One day there was a bit of a flap on, a message had been sent in clear instead of in code, Numerous officers were running around as if they were chickens waiting for their heads to be cut off, but it turned out O.K. for it was found that the Intelligence Officer was to blame and that the message had not meant much, so no harm could have been done.

We had some really good concerts there as you may well expect with the type of moneyed officers we had, and one night I was sitting there and having a good time when I received a pat on the back and Flynn the Drill Sgt. said 'Are you a musician?' I said 'No, what's wrong?' and he replied 'You'll be one in the morning if that hair of yours is not cut'. Well, you could have knocked me over with a feather, where was I to get a haircut at 10 p.m. or thereabouts. Old Charlie came to the rescue; he did a job on me with a pair of scissors and a razor. It passed Flynn's inspection but he said 'If your hair wasn't cut this morning I was going to present you with the company fiddle'.

After a while the whole brigade was on the move, H.Q. went to Breton Hill, Weybridge, the Guards went to Byfleet and the surrounding area, the Royal Norfolk ·Regiment went to Weybridge proper and H.Q. Coy. to Oatlands Mere, our Battalion H.Q. being in Weybridge proper.

Our H.Q. at Breton Hill overlooked Vickers Works near the old race track, and one day we were coming in from manoeuvres, marching along, troops, lorries, the lot, all in one big line. We were slightly under the trees at midday and had to pass Vickers Works, when suddenly we heard a great roar and we all dived for cover. It was a German aeroplane, and it dropped a bomb right on the machine shop of Vickers. The blast from the bomb took my breath away. Several people were killed in the workshop that was hit, luckily not as many as expected for it was lunch time and nearly all were out getting a few minutes of fresh air. I helped carry some of the people out, but did not stay long as we all had to be back with our units. I think the pilot of the plane was after us, for our column was about a mile long and he must have seen us in the trees. It was luck, I am sure, that this vital factory making Wellingtons was hit.

67

On the day of the bombing we had passed through West Byfleet, where the Welsh Guards had their Guard Room beside the main road, and as we passed, we being an armed party, their Guard turned out and gave the usual salute by presenting arms. I was carrying the Bren gun and being the front man I did not have to make an 'eyes left' but kept looking straight to the front on the command of 'eyes left!'. Next to me was a little shrimp of a chap, we called him Ack Ack Smith; he had something wrong with one eye so that it always looked upward. He made his 'eyes left' and then, to my horror, shouted to the sentry 'How'd you get in the army shorty?' Now to say this to a Guards sentry was beyond belief. They are always smart and have their wits about them, or so I have found, and how Smith could say this was beyond a joke. 'England's last hope' we used to call him; his equipment was just about on and his slung rifle was just about dragging on the road. I'm sure that if our officer had heard what Smith said he would have booted his behind.

While at Breton Hill we were issued with our first new battle dress. After the old service dress it appeared to me to be most comical, especially the front large pocket on the left leg. This did not seem to crease very well at first as ours had been dressed with anti-gas powder which made it stiff and showed white under the khaki. So I got rid of this by steeping the whole uniform in water for two days. After its immersion the battle dress became soft and pliable, and comfortable, far better than our service dress and also there were no buttons to clean. At first this uniform had to be buttoned to the neck, but with the advent of the Canadians who wore ties, they were also issued to us, with shirts from Canada. We felt really good and with a Canadian battle dress, which was a greener type of khaki, we were really smart. Puttees were done away with and web gaiters were issued, which only had to be blancoed daily.

I think it was on the 15th September 1940 that we got the order to 'stand to' as it was expected that we were going to be invaded. We sat about for forty-eight hours in our full battle order and dress. The canteen staff from the N.A.A.F.I. had decamped and we were just sitting there doing nothing. But things *were* taking place, and I am certain now that one of the chaps I knew had done the job, for when we stood down it was found that the canteen had been broken into and every cigarette had been stolen. We were without a canteen for about twenty-four hours, not

68

much, but during this time I asked one of the chaps for a cigarette and he gave me a brand new packet. I asked him where he had got his cigs from and he told me that there was a huge pile on the roof. Naturally at the time of the theft everywhere was searched, but someone had forgotten the roof.

Then we had a real fright, for Special Investigation Branch (S.I.B.) came to visit us. We did not know what it was about but we were soon to learn, for during the 'stand to' it was found that all the petrol had been interfered with and everyone had to say where they were on that day or during the forty-eight hours. Charlie and I were O.K. for we had been outside the Orderly Room all the time. It was the Motor Transport Section that got it and one man was taken away. It transpired that on filling the Brigadier's car up with what was thought to be petrol from a five gallon jerrycan, it turned out to be water and the vehicle would not start. Not only had that can been tampered with, but about fifty more had also been 'done'.

After the fright of the missing petrol I decided that I had had enough of being at Brigade H.Q. and asked to be transferred back to my unit. I got my transfer and was posted as a stretcher-bearer to 'B' Coy. not far away. There were five of us. Each day we had to report to H.Q. Coy. where the Band Sgt. was and to crown it all they decided to reform the band, a thing I dreaded, for I wanted to be a real soldier and serve with a Rifle Company. This was not to be, so I got on with it.

I had not been back with the band for more than a couple of weeks when we were informed that General Sir Peter Strickland, the Colonel of the Regiment, was coming to visit us. Well we really had a job on, whitewashing all the gateway entrances, sides of pathways etc., and we in the band had to practice all day long, all for a mouldy parade. This was held one day on the Green at Weybridge. It lasted for about two hours. The General was a real old soldier; he had been in the South African and World War One and he took his time, so by the time we marched off we all had cramp in our legs. He had also been Governor of Gibraltar while we were there, but fortunately he did not inspect us there. We would have all passed out in the heat.

One day on reporting at Headquarters Coy. one of the stretcher-bearer bandsmen was late on parade. We had a Sergeant Major Leeder then and he wanted to know why the bandsman was late and in reply P. said 'I've been looking for my embouchure'. Now this word means the way of putting the lips to an instrument to blow - P. played the clarinet - but the Sgt. Major not being a bandsman, P. was sent back to look for it! Didn't we laugh!

One day we marched from Weybridge to Walton-on-Thames, then to Epsom and then back to Kingston-on-Thames and Walton again, then after falling out at H.Q. Coy. I had, with the other four stretcher-bearers, to get back to our billets about two miles away. Foot inspection? We had no foot inspection, just laid down and went to sleep, awakening next morning cold and still with our boots and equipment on. At Kingston we stopped and lay down in the Market Place; there were plenty of people about, but they did not seem pleased to see us for we were all over the pavements.

About a week later with some others I went to Kingston for a stooge around and a rather stout pretty-looking girl asked if she had seen me the week before when 'all the soldiers were here'. I told her that that was possible and then forgot about it, for at that time I was not in the mood for girls. This girl, however, was the one I was to marry.

Why none of us were looking for a girl at the time was that we had a chap in our billet who went every night to Wimbledon, miles away, just to see a girl. Even if we had come in at 7 p.m. or 10 p.m. he still went to see her. We pulled his leg rotten and he used to really get wild and call us all sorts of names. It got so bad that he never had time even to help us with the cleaning of our billet. Sometimes he got back in the early morning, sneaking in without being seen, and in the meantime we had done his kit up and got his stuff ready for parade.

Well one night, after nearly a week of doing this lad's kit, Charlie and I got really fed up, so I got a four inch nail and put it through the heel of his boot and fastened it to the floor. Well, there was hell to pay. He knew it was us who had done the dirty deed, and it took him about two hours to get his boot clear. Afterwards he realized how browned off with him we were. He eventually married this girl, but none of us were invited to the wedding. There's no doubt at the time we were jealous, for he had been one of us prior to meeting her.

One night we got back late after a drunken spree and just laid down in our stupor and went to sleep. Suddenly I woke up. I could hardly believe my ears; a voice was calling the bottom rooms of the billet to attention. It was Saturday morning room inspection! I woke Charlie up, told him what was on, we didn't bother to wash, but got dressed, rolled every scrap of equipment we had in a groundsheet, stuffed it up the chimney, shoved our rifles up as well and cleared the billet, leaving our little room completely empty. We got away with it, and no one ever found out that we were missing. We sneaked back to the billet at about lunch time having been away for some four hours.

Every Saturday for some six months or more, and this is hardly believable, we marched as a band with the Battalion behind us from Weybridge to Camberley. There we drilled on the square of the Officers' Training College for about two hours, then marched back via Addle-stone. The rest of the day we had off.

They also took us in buses to Croydon where we dug into chalk and made miles of anti-tank ditches; we were told that this was where we would 'stand' if we were invaded. I suppose we were going to let them land and *then* beat them up, still the 1914 -1918 mentality, strategic withdrawals and all that.

During the winter of this year some bright spark at last thought up a scheme for us to experience battle conditions. The only snag was that we had to march all the way to Salisbury Plain; I know for certain that we passed Stonehenge. We bivouacked on the way, that is two of us made a small tent of our groundsheets and slept under them, but it was cold, and on the way it began to snow. When we arrived at the training area we didn't have to do any actual attacking, the Guards were doing that against us, but we had to lie out under hedges and later in the open, for we then had to crawl under a barrage which was fired so that it crashed down some fifty yards or so ahead. Then the barrage was lifted and we crawled some hundred yards or so and down the barrage came again. It shook the ground, and us, and took our breath away. No one was hurt, but this was real training, and *cold* - it was bloody bloody cold! I nearly cried, as we all did or felt like it, and to crown it all we had a 'mad' officer come chasing us every ten minutes or so. One time, we got the order to 'look front, stand to'. Well everyone got behind the hedge nearby, poked their rifles to the front and loaded with blank.

Being a stretcher-bearer and not having a rifle, I just lay under the hedge, and this officer shouted at me 'Stand to' and aimed a kick at my side. There was a right old din going on, so I shouted back 'How do you fire a bloody stretcher?' - good job he didn't hear me.

Our position was over-run, the Guards took us prisoner and we were marched off to the cookhouse to be fed. We didn't mind that; it got us out of the cold, but then we had another bright spark take us in hand and he marched us for three halts, that's about nine or ten miles, marching at about 3 mph. Suddenly we were halted by a despatch rider. We were told to fall out and it transpired that we had marched all the way in the wrong direction. Eventually an army bus came along driven by a civilian and he shouted at our officer (he was from the Norfolks) 'You must be bloody wet, you've got a load of lions there led by a bloody goat!' Our officer didn't half blush. We all got in the vehicle and were bussed all the way back to Weybridge, sleeping most of the way, dirty and extremely tired. When the driver of the bus got out of his vehicle he wasn't even five feet tall - he was the smallest driver I have ever seen. We gave him a cheer when he left, and so ended about four days of bloody murder. Little did I know that before the year was out nearly all the men I was serving with then, would either be dead at the hands of the Japs or killed in the invasion of Europe.

At weekends at Weybridge two things got our goat; one was the march to Camberley and back, and the other was that we sometimes had our free time stopped because we had to do exercises with the L.D.V. or Home Guard as it later became. They were mad. They would get really stuck in, fire blanks at us from about three feet and then charge at us with the bayonet. They were just like 'Dad's Army'. Getting taken prisoner was the best; they always appeared to have plenty of food, so we forgave them, for they always gave us a real good feed. We learned with them that it was better to be captured, we had such a good time. Soldiers are always good scroungers.

Another exercise we did was in Epping Forest. We went there by bus and drew enough tinned bully and cheese for two days. We had bread issued in the field and built our own little fires to make our own tea. Well one night with deep snow about, and only slit trenches to sleep in, Charlie and I got fed up, crossed what I suppose is the main A.11 now, and found a garage with an old car outside. It was open, so in we popped and went to sleep, keeping our rifles in the car with us.

Suddenly our Sergeant and Corporal opened the car door and yelled at us wanting to know what we were doing in the car. I informed them 'having a kip', at which I was told, along with Charlie, to get out of the vehicle and get back in our slit trench.

We dropped another clanger that night. Amid moans and groans we had to make another slit trench. It was bloody cold, but as we got down to hide from the bitter wind I said 'Bet the bloody Company Commander is in a billet somewhere the lucky sod,' and a voice from no more than a yard away said 'Who'd you think this is, thick mist? You nits!' Our Company Commander was in the next trench. He was a Capt. Read, and he was braving it just like his men. We looked up to a man like that.

Just when we were really digging in and getting to know the inhabitants of Weybridge, we were on the move again, this time to Hillingdon Park Camp, Hillingdon, quite near to the R.A.F. H.Q. at Uxbridge and not many miles from Northolt Aerodrome.

We had the usual camp, all bell tents, and it was wide open to the public; people used to walk through at all times till someone had the idea of putting barbed wire around our camp. When we tipped out in the morning to get washed, it was nothing to see several girls running fast to get out of the camp. The wire soon put a stop to that. The bell tents, believe it or not, held eighteen to twenty men, and all our equipment had to be in the tents at night, boots, pack and webbing (our pillows), groundsheet, palliasse and two blankets with our greatcoats as extra. The rifles were slung on the tent pole, the bayonet boss being clipped into a small sling so that the rifles, all twenty, were about eighteen inches off the ground, and our feet hit the pole at night. You can imagine what disorder took place if anyone wanted to go out during the night for a pee; rifles fell down, feet were hurt, but worst of all we lost our sleep. Well what we did eventually was pee in our boots, lift the tent flap and throw our boots out into the grass and collect them in the morning. No one ever lost a boot.

Northolt Aerodrome being nearby, we had the job of putting barbed wire all round it, mile upon mile, ton upon ton. We all had cuts and tears and were glad when the job was done. At that time there was no R.A.F. Regiment in existence or else they would have done the job for sure.

During this period at Hillingdon my right knee began to play up. I had hurt it years before when at Aldershot, having fallen out of a lorry, but it began to play up, so much so that I began to get on the other lads' nerves, for I could not keep in step having to drag my right leg. Having gone sick, I landed up in Hillingdon Hospital and had a semi-lunar cartilege taken from my right knee. It felt as though I had had my knee torn off. Every day it was looked at and when my leg was put down I all but screamed.

During my stay in hospital two things stand out in my memory. We had the usual run of casualties from London, burnt firemen and civilians. They teased me for being a short-term patient, for some had been there over a year, but one night a young lad who was a despatch rider at H.Q. was brought in. He had crashed in the blackout and was in a bad way. I recognised him as he lay on the bed in front of me, he was unconscious so I could not speak to him, so I went off to sleep. But during the night, at about 3 a.m., I woke with a terrific start. A bright flashing light seemed to blind me and this young lad shouted out 'Oh Mum please, oh Mum, they've killed me'. He then rolled his head and died. The nurse in charge of the ward ran over to him and, seeing that I was awake, told me that he was dead. In the morning I found that the lad's bed was empty and the day nurse confirmed that he had died. How his crash took place I don't know, but it shook me. He had been a good friend at H.Q., in fact we had swapped overcoats as we each liked the other's. He was a Scot and had been in the Royal Corps of Signals.

The other thing that I remember was that one day a young nurse came in to dress my leg and also give me a bed bath. I got the leg dressed, but when she took off my pyjama jacket she saw that I had tattoos on my upper arms. She said 'Are you a soldier?' I said I was and she ran out of the ward, and on returning told me that she was not going to help me any more as she was against war and all it stood for. As I was a soldier it was against her principles to deal with me. Thank goodness all the nurses were not like her. She looked daggers at me each day and I was glad to learn that I was being discharged, but didn't I swear, for I found on my return to the Battalion that I had been 'Y' listed and posted to the Depot at Norwich.

Chapter 7. Norwich

Before going to Norwich I was to report to Richmond Park Camp, Kingston on Thames, a convalescent camp where my leg would be treated.

From the camp I had to walk each day about a mile to the treatment centre at Kingston Barracks. That was bad enough, but each day we drilled without arms (rifles) and my leg began to swell like a balloon, till one day I went to the Kingston Barracks and there met Jack Lovelock the New Zealand runner. He nearly had a fit at the condition of my leg. Each day he massaged it and each day I was taken back to the camp by lorry; my leg got better and better.

As my leg improved I went out now and again in the evenings and at weekends. I was roughly a month at the camp and one Saturday morning I went into Woolworth's with a mate and there I met a shop girl named Clarice Clark. The lad I was with when I met Clarice was called Leslie; he came from somewhere near Audley End, Essex and was in the Essex Regiment. I made several dates with Clarice, then suddenly I was informed that I was having a week's leave and Leslie asked if I would like to go home with him. Having nothing better to do I agreed, but on getting off the train at Audley End I found that we had to walk about five miles to his home, right out in the wilds.

The next morning Leslie was gone. I asked about him and his mother told me that he had gone to see his girl at Kingston. Little did I realise that it was Clarice he went to see - I should have learned my lesson then, but I didn't.

Getting back from Leslie's home and into camp I learned that I was to go to my Battalion H.Q. at Wimbledon. (They had moved there from Hillingdon.) As soon as I arrived I found half of my kit missing. All I had left was just what I needed, no extras that I had accumulated. All those had gone - some thieving blighter had had a field day. So off I went to the Depot at Norwich.

Arriving at our Depot I was posted to Recruit Company with a Sergeant Major Haverson in charge. Being in Recruit Coy. was a real piece of cake for me, a bit irksome, but I was not going to complain, for all we did was drill, plus a hurried course of small arms firing. After a week or two I was called up to the Coy. Office and told that I had been promoted to Lance Corporal - me a Lance Corporal! I couldn't believe it. Some of the recruits moaned - they didn't have a chance with me for I knew the training backwards, and on being appointed I did the job to the best of my ability.

After a while I was given my own barrack room. The recruits were all men of about thirty-five to forty and a real bolshie lot led by a cockney who thought he was the 'cat's whiskers'. I knew I had a real handful to deal with.

The N.C.O.in charge of a barrack room is always up first, for he has to get everyone else up. Most of the men are up at the first peep of the bugle, others like a minute or two more, some want an hour if they can get it and I had got one of these, this cockney. One morning there he lay, still in bed, so I pulled the blankets off him and told him to get out of bed, and he said 'F... off!'. I nearly fell down at this retort and told him again; I got the same reply. The rest of the men were now looking and listening to what was going on, so I thought here goes, it's either him or me. I again pulled the bedclothes off him and told him to get up and I again got the same reply, so I got hold of him by the scruff of the neck and drove my fist straight into his face. At this he yelled like hell, put his boots on and in short pants and shirt ran down and out of the room telling me he was reporting me to the Sgt. Major for striking him. Now I knew I was likely to be in trouble for this and waited for the worst to happen. It did. Sgt. Maj. Haverson had been my Band Sergeant and stood no nonsense. What took place I don't know, but this man came back after seeing Haverson and reported to all and sundry that that bloody Sgt. Major had also hit him and told him to get back and dressed. After this episode I didn't have a scrap of trouble with any squad I had.

From Recruit Company I was transferred to Training Company which meant my moving from Nelson Barracks to Britannia Barracks, Norwich. Little did I know that this was to be a bad move for me in the end, and that I was eventually to lose my lonely stripe through no fault of my own.

Training was intense; we had to crowd into six weeks what would normally have been, in peace time, six months. Parades started at 7.30 a.m. after breakfast, but the day started much earlier when you consider that beds, rooms and breakfast had to be finished by that time. Out we went on to Mousehold Heath; first there was weapon training, then P.T., then recognition of aircraft, drill, everything that a soldier has to learn, especially in the P.B.I. - the Poor Bloody Infantry, without whom wars cannot be won.

We also went out on night exercises. The exercise I will now describe was at the time of the bombing of Coventry, and it really put the wind up me. We had got our platoon consisting of some thirty men, a Sergeant and an Officer, out of Norwich and into the flat area near Rackheath. We went over the ground during the day doing various exercises such as crawling, charging, and in general making us soldiers. The area was all meadowland with hedges and trees and there was plenty of scope for target recognition at night. We had full rations with us so there was no need to return to the depot for anything.

We had been warned to expect parachutists at any time so we were on the alert and my imagination was running riot. I had to take a tiny red light out with me and stay near it, and the troops had to advance in any way they could to this spot without being detected. If detected, a blank was to be fired in the direction of the advancing or crawling men. We were enjoying ourselves.

Well, off I went over several fields. Various N.C.Os and the officer went with the men, and after about half a mile I lit the lantern, but as I walked along I got the fright of my life. An enemy aeroplane went overhead, followed by others. I thought, trust me to be on my own on a night like this, for it was fine and clear, just the night for a drop of parachutists, and as I walked through a couple of meadows I heard behind me a shuffling noise. 'Sheeeee...' it went through the grass, and when I stopped so did the noise. This went on till I went to light the target light and there was still this noise now and again, so I got five rounds of blank out of my pouch, fixed my bayonet and shouted 'Come on you German bastards, I'll blow your guts out!' It was all heroic stuff, and me shivering in my shoes. I loaded and let rip with a blank and there before me, lit up by the flame of the blank from the muzzle of my rifle, was the enemy, a bloody herd of cows! The blighters had followed me, as cows and all farm animals will follow at night anyone entering a field. The whole episode had really put the wind up me I can tell you. I related what had taken place to the platoon and we all had a good laugh.

One day, up on Mousehold, we were doing an advance, with umpires assessing the recruits prior to their being posted. Well I got really posted that day. I was leading my section and we were told to charge at some low-down targets, supposed to be heads and shoulders of Germans. We had our bayonets fixed and I ran full pelt into my target and nearly broke my right thumb. Some clot, instead of fixing the target on a stick had put it in front of the stump of a telegraph pole. My bayonet went in O.K., but I came to an abrupt stop, nearly going head over heels, and after taking the bayonet off the rifle it took me about ten minutes to get it out of the wood.

I wrote regularly to my girl, Clarice, and even went to her home at weekends, all above board, there being no funny business allowed in those days. We got on all right, but I did not care for her dad, for he had not worked since 1918 and was living the life of Riley. Coupled with his pension, he had Clarice's money as well, and he couldn't abide soldiers. No member of his family had ever been in the forces, and certainly he hadn't - I should have been warned, but I was as blind as a bat.

We had most weekends off at the Depot, and as long as your platoon was not Passing Out, we were free of parades, so what I did was this :— I went to the Company Clerk, whom I had known in India and paid him five shillings, he gave me a Railway Warrant which I changed at Norwich Station for a ticket and I was off to Teddington where my girl lived. I must have been stark raving bonkers, for at times I would ring from Norwich at a pre-arranged time to speak to her and she would have forgotten and gone out with her cousin, who was guardsman mad. I should have known. I brought home pack upon pack of chocolates to her. I would buy other men's rations and even paid the cooks to give me some ham and meat to take home to help Clarice's family rations. I brought them lots of cigarettes which were easy to get in the army, and even took over guard duties or fire picket for seven and sixpence per night to save up so that I could dodge off and take her out. Now and again Clarice came to Norwich, I got her lodgings and she seemed to enjoy it up in Norfolk; she liked town life.

After about five months I was posted to the Battle School, High Leigh, Cheshire, and first attended a course from the school at the barracks in Warrington, I was there about three weeks learning communication, drill etc. and also about various gases. At the Battle

School we were taught officers' battle drill and the use of grenades, rifle and Sten Guns, Tommy Guns and mines. It was hard work and all exercises were done at the double. We were fit and well but we had the usual ration of idiots. One was an officer and he had been told time out of number never to kick a grenade which had failed to go off. This day we were firing phospherous grenades and one failed to go off. Like a clot, having thrown the damn thing, he ran up and kicked it. Being a Captain he should have known better. His screams could be heard for miles; we couldn't do anything for him but held him down till the ambulance came. We never saw or heard of him again.

Another clot was one of the instructors; he certainly should have known better. He was my senior instructor. We were sitting on ammo boxes from which we were getting out grenades; they had not been primed, so we had to fit both fused and combined detonators by first removing the base plug of the grenade. The thing looked like a small pineapple and fitted into the hand easily, the Mills type. We were getting on with priming the grenades with three and five-second fuses, when suddenly this clot of a Sergeant made as if to throw one. Up came his arm, the small handle at the top flew and instead of falling some fifty yards or so away it dropped at his feet. We all ran, me the fastest of the lot. I lay down and waited for the bang. Instead there was nothing, and there stood this bloody Sergeant laughing with his hands upon his hips. He thought it a huge joke; what he had forgotten was that any one of us could have dropped the grenades we were priming and the whole lot would have gone up, killing several of us. The officers didn't half dress him down and he left the school next day. I never saw him again.

Actual battle drill was the best; we went up into the Pennines through Manchester and somewhere above Derby and blasted into derelict cottages on the hillsides, using live ammo. Each platoon was split in two so that while one kept the alleged enemies' heads down, the other moved off to get a better position. Having got to a better position, the other section moved off till we all charged together and 'took' the cottage or house. It was all good fun, but using live ammo we had to be very careful, for we had men in the cottages who fired back into our area. We usually stopped firing about twenty-five yards away from the objective in case of accident. Remember we were firing both rifle and Bren from the hip.

We taught how to capture houses; we would surround the

objective, four or five would charge into the house and upstairs, while the rest waited under cover outside. The object was to clear the top floor, and the ground outside was held to be the 'killing ground'. As the enemy ran out of the house they were to be killed, no prisoners, for this was supposed to be in the heat of battle. Why we didn't clear the ground floor first I don't know, but I guess it was that the ground floor men were not going to fire through the ceiling in case they hit their own men. We were teaching a new army and I think we did a good job.

Every Saturday morning, along with the trainees, we did a ten mile 'run and walk' exercise by compass through the lanes of Cheshire and on return to the school we had to go to the thirty yards range and fire at a small twelve-inch target; any misses meant no weekend. We didn't do anything at weekends, but we were not allowed out.

Naturally all good things come to an end. I got shot during an exercise, right across the palm of my left hand; it didn't hurt at all at first, then came the pain. We were exercising with paratroops near Mostyn Hall and, feeling pretty rough, I pulled off my pack, found my water bottle and poured the water over my head so I didn't pass out. A Para Officer came along, poured some white powder on my hand and I was whipped off to hospital near Chester.

After a week or so I returned to the Battle School, but all the courses for the time being were finished, so I had to return to my own unit at Norwich. When I got back to the Depot, lo and behold a Bandmaster had arrived and, without any warning, I was posted back to the band, no stripe nor anything. I was browned off. I tried to get out of the band innumerable times. I asked the B.M. to let me go - not a chance. The Company Officer and the C.O. gave me the same reply, so I gave up.

One day in June 1944 I saw hundreds of planes and gliders passing overhead in the direction of the North Sea; the Invasion was on. I was extremely lucky for all the stretcher-bearers of 'B' Company of the 1st Battalion were killed or wounded on landing. I had missed that just through having a cartilege out, but now that I was graded A1, I wanted to be in France with the lads.

During my stay in Norwich, the city was bombed three times. I had been on Fire Watch each night and saw the city burn. There was no Ack Ack on the first night, a little on the second, but on the third night all hell broke loose. Rockets had been brought up and were fired directly over Britannia Barracks. What a row! It was like tearing paper multiplied a thousandfold. We didn't have any more raids. The centre of the city had been gutted. Prior to the bombing, rumour had it that Norwich could not be seen from the air at night - the raids put paid to that fallacy.

During one of these nights I found a young lad missing from the Watch. He had been outside when the raid began but he wasn't there now, and, search as we did, we still didn't find him till just before 'stand down' when we saw him crawl out of the ammo dump in the middle of the drill square. He had gone to sleep during the raid - what a place to hide!

During the next month the band went to the Tower of London where we stayed a week, playing at various places in the capital. On the way back we had a real do at Norwich Thorpe Station. Our carriage was in the station, but about two out. It was dark and our Band Sergeant stepped out of the carriage on to the track and nearly broke his neck. The air was still blue over this incident when, as we unloaded, young W. got his double B flat bass out of the guard's van and laid it down on the track side. The train shunted, the lip of the bell of the instrument caught an obstruction and the nipple at the bottom of the bend caught the grease box of the carriage. Crunch! went the double B; it was squashed till it was only about two foot six inches in size. We laughed, but when the B.M. saw what had taken place he soon removed the smiles from our faces; W. got seven days for that incident, and the damage caused.

We had a bandsman who was nicknamed 'Snakes', and if ever there was a dimwit as regards other people it was him. What he had been doing was living with another man's wife, a soldier who was out in Egypt or so he thought. She had had a child by 'Snakes' and he even lived out with her till one morning he came in all beaten up. Both his eyes were swollen and he could hardly move his back or arms; he was a wreck. We asked what had taken place for we could see that he had had a good hiding and we wanted to know the details. Out they came. The woman's husband had returned the night before, caught them in bed and also found the child. He had really gone to town on his wife and on 'Snakes'. All 'Snakes' had to say was 'He wouldn't listen to reason, I tried to talk to him and I couldn't make him listen!'. Considering where the soldier had found him we were not surprised. Later he went on parade on Guard Mounting practice, having forgotten one gaiter, and then, when sloping arms, his bayonet dropped off. He was well and truly in the mire. Next day he got seven days, but it didn't cure him. Snakes was a well-educated man of some thirty years. He had won a gold medal for organ-playing at St Andrew's Hall, Norwich and was a wizard on the piano. Women fell over each other to speak to him; he danced well and was a real snake-hips.

Now Snakes was not a regular soldier. (By now the band as such had few regulars, for most had either been captured in France at the retreat to Dunkirk, or were spread about all over the world. Some were Commandos, others in the R.A.F. and some were even Royal Engineers.) Snakes hadn't the faintest idea of discipline; he drove the N.C.Os potty. He was well-educated but just could not keep his eyes off women, they were his prey. He had been married once and blamed Hitler for this as his wife had wanted to be married before the 1939 War broke out. Anyway he was divorced now, which in those days was a novelty to us. He was a linotypist on a daily paper, but was on permanent nights,

One day, just prior to going abroad again, we went to New-market to play. As usual Snakes was missing when we got on the lorries to go. He was a clarinet player, of which we had more than enough, but he was missing and our B.M. was furious at being made to wait, for he wanted to be off. Well we got to Newmarket all right, and there stood Snakes waiting for us; he had come by train, but it didn't stop him from getting three days for being missing from parade. When we found him, he was talking to some Military Police who were entraining for abroad. Their wives were giving them a tearful farewell, but that night Snakes was kipping out with one of them. We asked him how he had got on and he told us he was getting his own back on the M.P.s - he thought it a huge joke.

During the course of my stay at Norwich Depot, Clarice and I decided to get married, which we did at St.John's, Hampton Wick. A friend of mine acted as best man and both Charlie and George attended. As I walked into the church, I said to my friend Ernie, 'Come on, let's go, I don't think I'll get married'. Well Ernie didn't agree with that, so in I went and got the job done. My mother was there, as one would expect, but after the reception she said, 'However did you get mixed up with this family?' I told her not to be nasty, but as it turned out she must have had second sight. Another week and I would have been on the high seas and could not have got married, so here's another who blames Hitler for his marriage. I must have thought I was going to be left on the shelf. I was twenty-four years of age.

Chapter 8. Foreign Parts

In early October 1944 we were informed that we were going overseas. We did not know whether it was France, the Middle East, or India. Off we went one night, leaving Norwich Thorpe Station on a locked train. Our next stop was at Newcastle upon Tyne, my home town. We were not allowed off the station and M.P. Guards stood all around us for we had been joined by other units. There was no running away; if anyone wanted to then they had *had it*.

The ladies at Newcastle treated us proud, teas, pork pies, cakes and, best of all, we got forty cigs each off them; the old saying that 'it's warmer up North' had really come true. We cheered them when we were leaving.

Locked in again, we arrived at Glasgow and got on to our boat, a real troopship this time. I forget it's name, but like all the rest, it was like a sardine tin. Some of the lads had never seen a troopship, never mind having been on one, and what a shock it was to them. Some did not understand why we did not have beds to sleep on, others why there were no dining rooms separate from where we slept. Having as usual made sure I was not mess orderly, I found a nice spot on the top deck to park my carcase.

After loading up, the ship set sail; it was a Friday. Those who were superstitious said it did not bode well for our voyage. Wherever we were going, we did not get far, for within an hour or two we stopped and anchored right in front of Greenock and stayed there a solid week. Some were even sea-sick on that little jaunt.

Then one night, the engines started up and we were off. It took us four weeks to get to Salerno, Italy, passing through the Straits of Gibraltar at night. We were a fast convoy and had sailed without escort till a couple of destroyers came alongside and were with us all the way till landfall. Of the voyage little can be said. Nothing was done at all; we just lay about, did our lookout duties, or played cards or Crown and Anchor. One bright spark cut our hair and got sixpence for his trouble. This was quite a lot considering there were close on a thousand men aboard ship. He used to boast about how much cash he had, and how the kit bag he kept it in could not be entered as he had a lock and clasp of brass fitted through the rings at the mouth of the bag. On the day before we landed he packed all his gear away, and next morning lo and behold all his cash had gone. Someone had cut the bottom out of the kit bag during the night. The mystery of the thief's identity was never solved.

To give an idea of how we were, I would say that we thought ourselves typical soldiers. We were all the same; anyone who did not swear on joining us certainly did after a while, it just couldn't be helped. We lived in filth and talked filth, but got on with the job with very few grumbles. We were good soldiers and that's not blowing my own trumpet. Anything we could scrounge or thieve we did, not amongst ourselves, that was not done, but we raided cookhouses and bulk supply depots, sold blankets, tobacco, cigs, and anything we could lay our hands on for the common good. Wellington, the hero of Waterloo, did not think much of our Regiment. He thought we were good soldiers in every way, but called us corrupt as it was alleged that while fighting in Spain our lot had sold their Bibles for money. I don't think he was far wrong - we weren't a load of cissies.

We stayed on the beach at Salerno for some two weeks. We were over-run by mice, but we managed to get rid of them in the most ingenious way. 'Snakes' thought up the idea and I have used it since - it never fails. He got a piece of wood, plus a large stone about eighteen inches high, which he put in the middle of the marquee we were in, laid the wood on the stone with the end poking over like a spring board, with a pukall (a canvas water bucket) underneath it. At the end of the wood he put a piece of paper with a little bit of cheese, just enough so as not to bend the paper. The wood, paper and cheese now hung over the pukall; the mice went for the cheese and the paper bent, and into the water they went and drowned. We caught hundreds that way, and used to have bets as to how many would be caught during the night, never less than ten.

I took no part whatsoever in any battle in Italy. I would love to be able to say that I did, but for the front line soldier it was hell on earth, for the country is very mountainous and mountains overlook roads - there wasn't a safe one anywhere.

While in Italy we stayed at Salerno, Naples, Cascerta, Cancello, Bari, Brindisi, Termoli, Foggia, Benevento, Forli, Monfalconi, Udini,

Padua, Pagani, Ferrara and other cities along the Adriatic which are now holiday resorts, like Rimini, Grado, Trieste, Florence and Perugia. In Sicily we were at Catania and Reggio, then went by cattle truck to Naples where we were when the Post Office clock blew up, there being a booby trap therein. We visited Pompeii and the surrounding area including Capri.

Christmas was spent in Naples on the Via Roma, and although did we get a Christmas, it was marred by the Church Army. We had amassed a good bit of money in the funds for a real good dinner, extra to what the army was allowing, and dinner was to be at 2 p.m. Well we all went out on the juice; I liked Vermouth which was only two lira a glass and most of us were quite merry when we returned to our billets. We had left Italian ex-prisoners cooking our meal, under the watchful eye of the Church Army, but when we returned there was no dinner. Well a riot broke out, and it landed up with one of our lads getting a week's field punishment. The C.A. had given our meal to the Italians! The lot was gone, vanished, not even a piece of pud left. We ended up having bully beef sandwiches. That was Christmas 1944.

During this period we visited Florence to broadcast over the Army network, this was done, but on leaving the building I heard someone cursing at an Italian, every rotten swear word in the book was being used, including several I had never heard before. The voice was Scottish, and when I went to see who it was I had a real shock, it was an Army Padre! I couldn't believe my eyes. Even I was shocked - so much for Army Padres.

At Padua we were billeted in a partially-demolished building. Next door there appeared to be quite a lot of toing and froing; police were taking people away at all hours of the night. We learned that these were captured Fascists, and they were being taken away to be shot.

Crossing the River Po was an experience. The main crossing was a Bailey bridge which the South African troops had built in twenty-four hours. There was a huge notice on the front telling us this, and also a notice saying 'This bridge cost lives, mind your bloody spacing'. Lorries were kept about twenty feet apart while crossing the river here, but we did not use this bridge but a small pontoon and as our lorry went over the middle pontoon the back dipped and our tailboard went under water. That shook us up, but the lorry held its grip and we got safely across.

At Forli two memorable incidents took place. First, an Italian

The band playing at Padua

ex-prisoner was boasting in English to some of our men about his conquests in the Southampton area. He was a real lover boy and looked it. Suddenly, after he had mentioned a girl's full name, a great bruiser of an R.E. went up and gave him such a wallop and knocked him out. We didn't understand until the R.E. said 'He's been talking about my sister, the bloody wop.' We left it at that. The second incident was when some Italian tried to sell some army stores belonging to our Army. We tipped the stall up and ran; half the town was after us, and if we had been caught I am sure we would have been knifed.

In Italy we could get anything for a tin of bully, even sex, but that was taboo to me; every street the length and breadth of Italy had a warning in English 'BEWARE V.D.'. Little boys were continually coming up to us and telling us that their sisters would be O.K. I booted several for I had a fear of V.D. and have so now.

The language was a difficulty to several of us. Some lads picked it up as easy as pie, but I didn't. I knew how to ask where to go for a certain street, but that was my lot. I also discovered the difference between words denoting work and wash.

At Forli there was to be a big parade where several men were to be decorated, so we had to get out our instruments and clean them up. Our double basses had to get their white covers cleaned and, with a tin of bully, Donk W. decided he would get an Italian woman to do the job. He did and landed up with seven days for his trouble. He duly handed over the big cover to be washed white and waited, and waited, and waited, but the woman did not return the cover. Eventually he found her washing the step outside a house near our billet and asked her where the cover was. Smiling broadly, she pulled out a filthy rag from her bucket and said 'Si, Si, labore'. Well Donk went spare. He kicked her up the bum, but it *was* his fault and it *wasn't*. He should have told her 'Lavare' meaning to wash. What annoyed him was the fact that he had given her two tins of bully beef. What he got was seven days for being 'dirty on parade'.

During this time I got a few letters from my wife Clarice, and then they stopped. It was terrible; I used to parade at mail-call and each time, no mail. This went on for months and when I did get a letter I was told that she was busy and it was a hard job to write. I was potty, I used to write every day. At last I decided two could play at that game and didn't write any more till I got to Vienna which was some considerable time later. I went out and got drunk.

While on the east coast of Italy we were attached for a few days to the Long Range Desert Group; they were raiding Yugoslavia at the time, and there were several girl soldiers from that area with them. We went right up a mountain one night into a big barn for a beer-up; they had promised us one and we had a real do, but before we started I went outside with one of the L.R.D.G. men and saw a carpet rolled under a lorry. I asked if I could use it to sleep on - it was deep snow outside and bitter cold. I was told that I could and unrolled it and out popped a dead British soldier; I soon rolled him up again and didn't ask any more. I got laughed at by the other men of the unit who were a real tough lot; nearly all had beards and looked like out-of-work pirates. It appeared that the lad in the carpet had been wounded on the way back from the patrol, and had died; they were taking care of the matter next day.

One night, on a road block, we had cause to stop a large lorry loaded with corn and I got the surprise of my life. I asked the driver to get down out of the cab which he did, but instead of having a hard time trying to get him to understand me, out it came in a broad Norfolk accent. He had been deported before the war, and was one of a family of Italians who lived in Norwich. Two other things took place that night. A set of wheels from an anti-tank gun disappeared; they were there one minute and gone the next. The next thing was that a tank was stuck in a ditch nearby. Not only was it stuck, but it was out of petrol as well. However, it was fuelled up and it was decided that the tank would get itself out of the ditch. There was a bungalow nearby, so chains were put right round this building and the tank began to pull. So well did it pull that, the chain went right through the place and it all collapsed in ruins. This was just outside Bologna.

On one of our visits to Florence, or Firenze, as the Italians call it, I was stopped by a young woman. My mate and I were out for a walk and this girl, she really was a beauty, stopped us and speaking in perfect English asked if we would buy a lottery ticket for the re-building of Italy. I was in one of my moods, browned off with everything and everyone, so without hesitation I said 'Re-build Italy, you must be joking, scram!' She looked at us dumbfounded, but I believe that day I had heard from my wife to say she had been bombed out and I think she wanted me to come home. Fat chance! I went and saw an officer and asked if it were possible and all he said, and I didn't blame him, was 'Who hasn't?'

After Florence we went all over southern Italy, and one lad in particular was really not with it. If anything went wrong he called it a 'Damned C.B.' meaning 'colossal balls-up', we often chided him over this and asked why he didn't come out with it properly if that was what he meant. Anyway before long he was worse than anyone. He had had an excellent education and was a real good lad, we all liked him, but boy, did he learn to swear!

On returning to Florence, we learned that the war was going to end before long. We took that with a pinch of salt, but suddenly there was every Italian wearing a red scarf. We had not seen them before and were told that these were 'partisans'. Prisoners were coming in off their own bat and were being marched in the direction of the salt marshes near Rimini.

One morning an R.E. officer came to our billet in Florence which was on the Via Cavour, not far from the cathedral there, and told us that the war was going to end that day at 11a.m.

Now you would think this would bring great rejoicing. Not on your nelly! We were sitting round against the wall having our breakfast, and there was a dead silence. It was taking time to sink in. The officer left - he didn't appear to be too concerned - then suddenly a man got up.

He must have been overcome with patriotic fervour, for there was an old piano in the room we sat in and he went straight to this instrument and began to play 'Land of Hope and Glory'; well he got the first five or six bars out when suddenly a soldier from the Inns of Court picked up a boot and threw it. It hit the piano player at the back of the ear and he went out like a light and fell to the floor. No one bothered, and it took several hours for the fact to sink in that the war was over in Italy - we finished one day before the B.L.A. in France and Germany. I often think of that lad who played the piano - no one seemed to care a toss.

The war having ended, it might be assumed that we went back to a real cushy life. Not a bit of it! There was a whole lot of clearing up to do and the German Army to be disarmed. The line had finished at Ferrara and the Germans were put into units and had either to march or travel by lorry to the salt marshes over on the Adriatic side, but there was a snag. Having failed to beat the Germans in war, the Italians decided that they could now take pot shots at them. The Germans were going to the designated areas allotted to them quite peacefully without escort, but the Italians nearly caused another war! The upshot was that British troops were sent to guard them, in fact some of our soldiers in our area were attacked by the Italians and the Germans got out of a lorry and beat them up and helped our lads to clear them away.

Hostilities being over, the British Army bands were reformed and we went to Udine; we stayed for a few days then pushed on to Mestre where we went into a Transit Camp. Everyone was bolshie, no one appeared to be in charge, meals were going all day and it was a real mess! Then thankfully we were sent along the Causeway at Mestre, where huge signs stated 'Benito Finito', or 'Benito Caput', to Venice where we got on 'ducks' and were sent to the Lido for two weeks' rest. What a rest! The sun was fine, the sands glorious, the hotel was being run like a hotel, we had tea in bed, and maids to wait on us. Our every whim was catered for, swimming costumes were issued and we just lay on the sands and stunk.

What the Italians in this part thought of us I cannot imagine, for the war did not appear to have affected them, and what they thought when we first got to the hotel I dare not think, for each bed had a pure white counterpane on it and we just jumped on to the beds, equipment and all, and laid on them. It was heaven, but we did make a mess of both the beds and the rooms. Rifles that were put against the wall slid

Our hotel in Venice

down and marked the beautiful walls, boots scraped the floors and we made it a mess, but eventually the fact dawned on us that we were human beings and what we were doing was not on. Gradually everything changed and we took a real pride in keeping our rooms clean and tidy instead of fag packets and grape pips, orange peel etc. on the floor, we went really all out and made everything grand.

The hotel had been the playground of the Fascists and had the emblem of the bundled sticks and axes everywhere. It was as luxurious as the Hilton is today, just our luck, us poor soldiers enjoying it, we felt so upset!

During the period we were at the Lido I went back to main Venice and walked all over the place. St Mark's Square was where our N.A.A.F.I. was, right in the far right hand corner looking from St Mark's. I have never been back, but we didn't really appreciate where we were. All we thought of was getting home. How that turned out for me I shall tell you later.

One day we were told to push on towards Monfalcone, about half way between Venice and Trieste. We stayed in a big hall the first night and got a real fright. In the middle of the night there was a huge explosion, a hidden ammo dump left by the Germans had blown up. Some Italian

90

Partisans were foraging for ammo and weapons, and one of them had gone in with a lighted candle. Bang! the whole lot had gone up. Bricks, shell-cases and numerous other objects fell on to our building. We thought it was Tito shelling us, for as usual the Allies had fallen out and the Jugoslavs weren't having any of us. Anyway we left that day and went into Trieste which appeared to be very little damaged. We stayed in Trieste about five weeks. Some were billetted near an old race course. The gates to this area were not wide enough to get our vehicles in and out with ease, so we got some American soldiers to clear a big mound outside the gates and take them down. It took them about two hours, the very first time I had ever seen a bulldozer and how it worked. It was a real eye-opener to us, for its use saved hundreds of man-hours with pick and shovel.

After Trieste we were ordered back to Udine and one night we stayed on the road, just near a peach orchard; the trees were laden, we couldn't believe our eyes. There was a gate to the orchard, so in we piled. I got a blouse full, but on coming out I saw a notice and nearly fell down dead. The notice showed a skull and crossbones with 'MINEN' written beneath; either the whole area was mined or the Germans had put the sign as a joke to stop us having the peaches, probably the latter, for there were about forty of us and surely someone would have trodden on one during our rushing about in the trees.

At Udine my mail caught up with me, about four letters from my wife, one of which told me that it was time I was home and if I didn't come soon I need not return at all. Thank you very much, I thought. Another letter, which I read out to the lads, encouraged me to go on strike as perhaps they would send me home then! Clarice had a job with London Transport now and it was all right for them to strike, which they had done during the war, but the Army called striking *mutiny* and that just wasn't on. From then on my letters were few and far between. I wrote about every two weeks and I even sent parcels home, but I was told 'I don't like this and I don't like that', so I stopped.

We moved up the Brenner Pass into Austria after a while, stopping first at Klagenfurt, then at Bruck where we met Russian soldiers for the first time. They stopped us, but did not search, as later they did. We were put into a huge building which had been a P.O.W. Camp. The beds were three-tier bunks, which looked O.K., but as soon as we got into them they fell apart; we ended up sleeping on the floor. Next day we went by train to Vienna which by then had been split up into zones, British, Russian, American and French. We were allocated Meidling Caserna and were attached to the Dorset Regiment; they had got there before us and had the best of the buildings. The Russians had had them before and they had used everywhere for a toilet; corners were all fouled up, tops of stairs, any room had been used and it took us about a week to clean up the mess. In Vienna the people were frightened of us. They thought we would be like the Russians who had really gone to town and flattened huge areas of the city. It was alleged that they had raped and pillaged on entering the city, and honestly who could blame them after what the Germans had done to them. I don't think they'll ever forget.

The streets of the city had huge, orderly piles of rubble right down the centre. Even the palace of Schonbrun had a dirty big shell hole through the left front. All the trees were gone, cut off about two feet from the ground and the people looked dead as they walked about. Mind you, a great part of the city was untouched, especially round about the Opera House and the Rathaus or parliament buildings. Karlskirk was untouched as was St Stephen's Church, all land marks in the city. They had actually got off very lightly compared to London. Some of the big buildings, though, looked as if a field gun had been fired from one end to the other; they were a mess.

Of all the Allies, the Americans appeared, to be the ones the Austrians disliked most; they had done the night bombing and flattened a considerable number of houses on the outskirts. What Austrians I knew later always complained of them and their bombs.

Rations in the city were very poor. In the Russian Zone there was very little, they got no meat. The French were a little better, so were the British, but the American Zone was provided with plenty. This caused a lot of discontent with the populace, but one could not really blame the Russians and the French. They had suffered and knew what war really was; they had won and they were showing the Austrians who was master. The Russians hated the Austrians because a lot of them had fought at Stalingrad, and the Austrians moaned because many of their menfolk had been taken prisoner there.

Now that we were in barracks we gradually reverted to peace-time soldiering. Spit and polish was again the order of the day. The Russians and the French were real heaps. I didn't see an American unit at all; they were there, but where I don't know. I had had enough of them in Italy when we were attached for about two weeks to the fifth Army H.Q. Their moaning about no ice-cream etc., gave us all the pip, and as for their equipment, well I think each man had his own jeep to carry his kit!

About this time several men who were a lot older than I, were sent home via Villach in Austria. I was told I was in 25 group which was not too bad, but we had two blokes, one from Peterborough and one from Felixstowe, Suffolk, who were a real pain in the neck. Everyone was trying to save up, but they didn't half overdo it. The pair of them used to buy a cup of tea in the canteen for five pfennigs and the two of them halved it, one drank out of the saucer and the other had the rest of what was left in the cup. Now is that saving up, or is there another name for it?

The band played all over the city, and the tune the Austrians liked best was the Radetski March. They clapped and clapped and some even cried; they may have been crying over the way we played it, but I don't think so.

In the course of my roaming the city, looking at all the old buildings and what was left of the parks, I was out one night with one of my mates and fell in with a lovely-looking girl. It turned out that her name was Hildegarde, and from then on I used to see her about three times a week. She introduced me to her family; her father was a chemist and her brother was a priest. She was good fun and took me to the opera and the theatre where I saw 'Tosca' and 'Land of Smiles'. I learned there that one of the songs we always sang in the canteen 'Roll out the Barrel' was of Austrian origin. We also went for long walks in the country in the American Zone and had a really good time. My troubles at home were forgotten and I thought it would be a good idea to stay in Austria, but then felt I couldn't really, for despite the differences with my wife I had made a bargain and I had to stick to it - we did in those days.

One night I went to the pictures with Hildegarde, and a film showed all about the concentration camps. As a man, the whole audience stood up and shouted 'Propaganda!'- they just didn't believe it or didn't want to. If looks could have killed, both Hildegarde and I would have been done there and then.

Now Snakes had decided that he wanted to stay in Austria; he wanted to marry an Austrian girl. He told the local priest that he had army permission and produced a paper to him saying so. It was a clever forgery which he had made himself, but when he asked for army permission properly, thinking he had got over the civil bit, the priest had already reported the facts to the army and into clink Snakes went. Romeo had nothing on him, nor had Casanova, he just had to have a woman to live with.

At first when we had got into Austria there was a 'No Fraternisation Order'; this lasted about two weeks. There were plenty of A.T.S. and V.A.Ds. about, but no one would look at them. Concerts were even arranged for men to meet the A.T.S. and hardly anyone went to them. We had seen enough of khaki and enough's enough.

Chapter 9. Discharged

Came the day when my group went up for discharge. I told Hildegarde and that brought the pains on. She knew I had a wife, and I said goodbye to her at Vienna Main Station. She was crying like anything. I did write to her once, but didn't put my address on the letter; it was better that I didn't. I have never been back to Austria; she would be about my age now, in her seventies.

I went to Villach to start the journey home. All excess uniform and weapons were taken from me, also my Vienna pass which was written in all the languages of the Occupying Powers. I retained a German steel helmet and an S.S. dagger I had found.

At Villach I was told that I looked too young to be in twenty-five group. I nearly went spare. Of course I was, I had been in the army for over twelve years! They decided to radio to London to find out the facts - back came the message for me to be discharged. Home I went via Innsbruck, Munich etc. to Calais.

Coming over, it was stated that all trophies of war were to be handed in or back we would go. Over the side first went my trombone, then the S.S. dagger; the latter I would have liked to have kept but the trombone I was glad to be rid of. I have never played a note since that day, and never wanted to. We landed at Folkstone.

Getting to our discharge area which was Aldershot, we were again examined fully and taken to Woking and issued with civvies. At least I got a pair of socks and a couple of shirts and shoes. There wasn't a suit to fit me, so my measurements were taken and I got the suit later. Some suit.

I went as far as I could by train to get to Teddington. I changed at Wimbledon thinking I could carry on to my destination, but found that there were no trains, so with my kit bag on my shoulder and my civvies in a box, I walked to Clarice's home at 88, Bushey Park Road, Teddington, arriving I remember at exactly 2 p.m. I had not written for a couple of weeks so they were not expecting me, but I was in no way ready for the greeting I got.

I knocked on the front door and a voice which I recognised as being that of my mother-in-law called 'Who's that?' I replied 'Me.' 'Who's me?' came in reply, so I called out 'Jack.' I got a real welcome then, 'What! You back already!' Cor, I thought, what a bloody welcome! That's what I got and I'll never forget it till my dying day.

Clarice was not at home for a start. I didn't think she would be, for bus crews had a forty-eight-hour working week and took their days off Monday one week and Tuesday the next. So I went off right away to Kingston Garage where she was employed and she was granted a week's holiday straight away. I thought that pretty good. She seemed happy to see me and it looked as if all was well.

I hadn't been home a couple of days when the 'old man' her father kept on about getting a job. He had quite a lot to say on that matter. He had even got a job himself while I had been away, but had been so lazy that he had allowed some housebreakers to break into the home of John Ford the film director during the day. He got the sack of course and didn't he think he had been hard done by. The fact of the matter was he had been in the local pub while the job was being done.

One day I went with Clarice to Gunnersbury Street Station to see if I could get a job on London Transport. I passed physically, but I was one and a half inches too tall. I was asked if I would like to drive a tram on London Embankment, but I declined; it was miles from Teddington. I stuck a month out of work, or on leave, for I was entitled to ninety-one days leave, one day for every month served abroad. I got £350 gratuity which I partially spent getting some civvies. All the money which I had saved during the war and had left with Clarice had disappeared. Then I bought some furniture, a bed and a tallboy plus a sideboard. The house was in a mess; first aid repairs had been done after the local bombing, but the walls were bare and the inside doors were off. It was a bloody mess. I asked about this and was told it was in hand, but it turned out that the thing had not been reported properly to the local council at Twickenham and they had no knowledge of the repairs that had yet to be done. I got that settled and eventually all was done. The old chap never gave one bit of a hand, he did nothing, just sat there and criticized the workmen until one of them told him off good and proper. I did the inside painting, all white, and after it was done and the stairs still wet, the old lady used a wet swab to clean some dirt off the wet paint, you can imagine the result. I had a real good do with a neighbour over her. I had just finished the bottom bay window of the house and was

96

admiring my handiwork when the old lady got up the steps to see what I had done. Putting two and two together and making five, the neighbour called me lazy for letting my old mother-in-law, who was about sixty-seven at the time, get up steps to paint. My mother-in-law didn't even tell her neighbour that it was me who had done the job, and when I told her, she said I had only done it for my own convenience. Wasn't I wild! I decided then that I was going back in the army, for Clarice didn't defend me in any way. I honestly believe now that they had hoped I would never come back from the war, they made me so welcome. All her friends had married Yanks, I think that was the trouble.

I sent away for the required forms to re-join and filled them in and was on the way to post them when I decided I wasn't going to let my in-laws beat me - I'd beat them and I did eventually. Had I re-joined then, in 1946, I would have gone to Korea, for that was where the First Battalion landed up in 1948.

After having a good long talk with my wife in Bushey Park, Teddington (I was unable to get out of the hearing of my mother-in-law otherwise) we decided to try and make a go of it. I got a job with my brother-in-law at the Hampton Court Gas Co., Hampton Wick, as a stoker. It was really hard work but it brought in £6.15s. per week which was good in those days, and for a while I was happy there, with Clarice's brother. He was married and had seven children, living in a two up and two down house near the works. His wife wasn't so hot and, liking his drink, he was never encouraged to stop by her, in fact just the opposite.

When I went to my first shift at the gas works I thought I was entering Dante's Inferno. The retorts were of the horizontal type and were fed by a huge machine. To look at, they were like a bake oven, but when opened showed a white hot sheet of heat; this was the coal which had been baked, twenty-five hundredweights at a time. There were some sixty retorts on our floor and each retort was baked for eight hours. Coke, gas, creosote, benzol and other products were extracted from the baked coal. When the retorts were opened the machine which fed them first pushed out the white hot coke into a running stream of water about two feet deep which was to the front of the mouth of the retort; the coke came out and was carried away by the water. After the coke had been extracted we covered the stream up. At first this appeared to me to be a very frightening process; it was hot, but not too bad, and I soon swung into the way of doing things. We also had to clean out the fires to these retorts, which were at ground level below, and we used to get about one hundredweight of clinker from them using a steel probe about ten feet long and two inches in diameter. It was really heavy and I soon got callouses on my hands, but the worst thing was the dirt. The coal dust got into the skin and, although we showered before going home at the end of the shift, I always had another wash-down at home.

I stuck this job for only about nine months for I fell out with my brother-in-law. His wife was supposed to save up his rent money for his home, and had a Post Office Bank Book for the job. What actually happened was that she spent the money and made an entry in the book as if she had paid monies in. My brother-in-law went to the Post Office to draw out this money, a year's rent, and when he produced the book to the cashier he all but got arrested; the entries were in, but no post office stamp, hence no money and as a result my wife, his sister, came to me knowing I had a bit saved up and asked me to help him. I let him have two hundred pounds which I expected to get back, but he made no attempt to repay this money, so the best thing I could do was get away from him by getting another job.

I applied through S.S.A.F.A. for a job and through them I began as a postman at Twickenham Post Office at the rate of £4.15s. per week, a princely sum. In the meanwhile Clarice was still working on the buses. She was earning good money, but I was paying her tax as well as my own; she thought that was wonderful. I kept £1.00 and gave her the rest. I didn't mind and we gradually saved up, the only snag was that I let her have the Post Office book in her name, I found out later how wrong I had been.

On my first day at the Sorting Office, Twickenham, I found that another bandsman, much older than I, was also there. He was a full postman while I was what is known to them as Temporary, which meant I was on probation and had not been made a Civil Servant Class 3. I worked from 5 a.m. till 11 a.m. and then from 5 p.m. till 9 p.m., split shifts, no overtime. We managed, for with the money Clarice brought in we were doing fairly well. She was getting between £9 and £11 per week, we paid her mum £4 and after tax had some £6 or more to play with and save.

Well, came the day about ten months after I was home that she was pregnant. Talk about make a fuss! I thought I had committed a major crime. Her mother and father didn't like it and didn't I get some black looks and snide remarks. I put up with it, but decided that I would go back to the gas works as now we would need to save more money. I joined the H.S.A. which was a godsend as things turned out.

I suppose Clarice had cause to complain, for just after I had come home I got drunk, and during the night I kept shouting out the name Hildegarde. She tackled me about this and I told her that she must have been mistaken and that I was calling out my sister's name, Hilda, (I hadn't seen her for years), but she didn't believe me.

Before I left the Post Office I found that there was another joker from our Regiment there. I had known him as a thief in the army and he'd had many a hiding from his comrades. It wasn't done amongst ourselves, Italian or German didn't count, they deserved it. He really was no good. Anyway I left and the Inspector wished me the best of luck. The reason for leaving I gave as the wages being too small, but really it was because, just before I left, I worked thirty hours overtime delivering telephone books and got the princely sum of £3.00! I had not left the Post Office many weeks before I read in the paper that our 'friend' had been arrested for stealing registered mail – it had to come.

Back at the Gas Company I was put in charge of the vertical retort house. Everything was automated here and the retorts were fed from the top. We had the same type of fires and it wasn't so dirty either. I got on really well with the workmen there, especially with a Welshman who helped in part to change my life.

In all types of work there is always danger, and one night when I had just clocked off, I looked up to the top of the retort house and I thought I could see a blue flame and went to investigate. There was a flame; escaping gas from the retorts had ignited the coal bunkers overhead, so I just pulled out a big hose and spent about an hour putting the fire out. It wasn't a fire with huge flames but just like a gigantic gas burner on low. Having put out the fire with no danger to myself I just noted it in the occurrence book, hour and date etc., with no frills; there was no damage and next day I had forgotten the matter, but on pay-day, Friday, I got £200 extra in my packet and a letter of thanks from the manager.

The same week I had another crisis in the retort house. We were going up by lift while there was a great thunder storm on and torrential rain. The lift stopped and the lights went out. My Welsh workmate didn't know anything about electricity; neither did I for that matter, I knew how to mend a fuse and that was it. I mended the light fuses which had blown and pulled out the left fuse and rewired it and began to put it back in, well, I got a terrific jolt through my right arm and landed up on my back about twenty feet away from the open door of the lift - the fuse box was wet inside. I learned my lesson that night - I would get an electrician in future.

During my spell with the Gas Company I got to know a Metropolitan Police Sergeant in T Division, Imber Court. He had got to know that I worked on shifts and someone had told him I worked O.K., so after a morning shift which I finished at 2 p.m. he offered me a job with him. He was moonlighting, knocking down old buildings for their bricks which we sold at £5 per thousand, and lead which we sold to a scrap metal dealer. We also made concrete paths for people. What was charged I don't know, but I used to get £10 for an afternoon, finishing at about 7 p.m. He used to pick me up from the Gas Company to go with him to work, and could he work, like a Trojan. He was a New Zealander married to an English girl, and they lived behind our house.

The bricks were knocked out and cleaned and they were collected by the buyers, but the lead we put in a Police Patrol Car and that was how we took it to the dealer. The money that was earned in this way was being spent on a house he was building. My employer in this enterprise had it all cut and dried; except for the use of the Patrol Car, all was above board.

I lost a week's pay while helping him out. He brought an old boy with him and asked him to remove the boards from a floor and throw them down. I knew this chap - he was stone deaf. One day, despite my repeated calls to him not to, the old blighter dropped a big timber down near where I was working. There were several little pieces of timber on the floor,and the timber coming down hit a smaller piece which jumped up and hit me on the top left jaw and cracked it. I was rushed to hospital and after X-Ray was allowed home. I just had a swollen face which didn't affect me much. I still lost a week at work, but was paid by my Sergeant.

In the meanwhile Clarice had a baby boy, we called him Brian. He was lovely and was born at Bearstead Nursing Home, Hampton Court. It made a real change to us and we were both very proud of him. I was speaking to my brother-in-law again by this time and we decided we would go into business together, cleaning windows etc. This was fully agreed with him, so I bought the ladders, two pairs, and had some bills made out. I decided we would quit our jobs and start some two to three weeks ahead. Then, trust my luck, my brother-in-law backed out. I burnt the handbills and I don't know where the ladders went. I decided there and then to leave Bushey Park Road where we lived and got the Welshman I worked with to call at Norwich City Police Station, Norfolk, and get me some recruiting literature as he was going on holiday to that city. This he did, and eventually I was called to Norwich, but I was unable to keep the appointment, for a retort blew up and some red hot coke dropped down my shirt, through my trousers and into my jackboots. I had a terrible burn on my leg, and I couldn't report like that, could I?

Eventually I did get an appointment at a County Police Head Quarters and I was lucky to be taken on, for I was within one week of my thirtieth birthday and thirty years was the maximum age. Anyway I got in and, without telling Clarice or her family, I got my cards at the works and disappeared. I wrote from the Training School telling Clarice what I had done and saying that in future I would be earning five guineas per week plus seven shillings Rent Allowance, plus a free travel warrant every twelve weeks. I can tell you it was a bit of a shock to them all for I had kept all this secret from the family. I was rid of my in-laws and had every chance of getting a house from the force.

About a week before I left the Gas Company to join the Police Service, I nearly got on the wrong side of the law, for on night shift there was another Welshman and during the night he disappeared for about two hours. I saw him go and thought nothing of it. I saw him again at 5.30 a.m. and he asked me if I required any paint brushes. I told him I didn't and had no use for them. I left it at that and went home thinking nothing of the matter.

At 10 p.m. the same night I reported for work as usual. The manager was there and told me that a friend of mine was waiting for me in his office. I told the manager I didn't have many friends, if any, at the works, but he told me this chap was a friend of his as well. I went up to the office and didn't I get a shock. I saw a great big hulk of a man sitting behind the manager's desk. I said to him 'I don't know you' and he replied that he knew me, so I asked him who he was, and to my surprise he said 'I'm Detective Sergeant...... (I don't remember his name) and I wondered what the hell he wanted me for. He informed me that there had been a burglary during the night at the works and asked if I know anything about it. I informed him that I certainly didn't, and then it hit me, that bloody Taffy I bet! He then asked if I had enough soap etc., and then suddenly said 'Are you short of paint brushes? I hear you're decorating your house'. I politely informed him that I was short of nothing and the last thing I would be doing was paint the house as it wasn't mine as I lived with my mother-in-law. He then asked if anyone had offered to sell me any paint brushes. At this I knew it was Taffy who had got me into this mess and I told him how he had been missing from the shift during the night and had offered me some paint brushes that morning. Saying 'Thanks', he told me I could go, and within the hour Taffy was being taken away in handcuffs. All the stuff stolen had come from the works main store; it was a rotten thing to do for we were well paid for those days and the management were tophole.

⬥✳⬥

Chapter 10. On the Force

On getting to Force H.Q., Norwich, I was examined and had an Educational Exam. That was a snip, for one of the Sergeants there had been in the army with me, so I got on all right. I was then issued with my uniforms, two helmets, flat cap, two greatcoats, two jackets and trousers, handcuffs, truncheon and numerous books. Then I was marched before the Chief Constable, he gave me and another man a real good talking to which took a whole hour. The last bit I remember from him was, 'Don't go out there and pick up the nearest village tart'. I thought this was funny because I believed I was joining the City Force; instead I had joined the County. I eventually got to the Magistrates Court, was sworn in, spent the night in the city and left on the Sunday with my travel documents for the Training School at Eynsham Hall, Oxford, and there began the best period of my life. I'd got a real job and I was proud to be one of the 'Thin Blue Line'. This was March 1948.

I arrived at Oxford en route to the Training School at about 5p.m. on the Sunday evening. There were about thirty young men on the train and it turned out that they were destined for the same place as myself. They came from all the Forces east of Gloucester, south of Lincolnshire and North of London. The Metropolitan had their own training school.

I met P., the lad who had joined with me, and after a few minutes we were met by an Oxford City Police Officer who guided us to a bus outside and, piling in, we were all brought to Eynsham Hall about seven miles from Oxford and near to Witney in that county.

We were given a really first class meal and then shown our rooms; some were single, others with about six persons. I got in with five others at the top of what was known as the grand staircase. The school was actually a great country house, oak-panelled and in first class condition, I was allocated to Course twenty-two with a Sergeant N. of Oxford in charge as our instructor. The grounds were marvellous, a real pleasure to wander round.

The whole place was run on military lines; we were told all about discipline, but this turned out to be a piece of cake after the army.

Both P. and a couple more besides myself were told not to wear our uniforms after the first parade next day, because they were too tight. So we didn't have to spend nearly half an hour brushing down before parades *and* we received ten shillings plain clothes allowance.

The first few weeks we spent learning definitions. It took me some time to get the hang of these, especially burglary and larceny - they appeared so long and complicated - but I did learn.

P.E. or P.T. was my forte. We had an elderly Sergeant take us for unarmed combat, and he used to really lay into the lads, in fact he was a bit of a bully. He didn't know that I had served in the forces and I didn't enlighten him either, till one day he picked me out to show how a man could be thrown and held on the ground. He had flattened one or two before me, so out I stepped and, instead of me flying through the air and landing on my back, I countered him and after he had got up he asked where I had learned the hold. I explained that I had been in the army for twelve years. He didn't bother me again.

They kept both our minds and bodies fit there with good food and plenty of time in the open air. It turned out I was the eldest in the class, and for that reason one day I was put in charge of the First Aid class while our Sergeant was called away. Having done First Aid as a stretcher bearer I could at least tell the lads what to do, but not what we actually did do. We were practising how to bandage up a person with a broken leg using a Thomas Splint, a long piece of wood about two or three inches wide, a quarter of an inch thick and three and a half feet long; there was a hole at the bottom end of the splint so that a bandage could be threaded through and secured to the leg. Well, just for a laugh, I put the splint on a chap's nose. His nose poked through the hole and the rest of the splint protruded forward. I then bandaged the lad's head and we were marching him round our instruction room when in walked the Commandant. He stood there open-mouthed. I think he was trying to deduce what work of art this was; then all of a sudden he yelled and asked who was in charge. I reported that I was. He didn't say anything, just walked out, but when our Sergeant came back he told me that I was on Commandant's Orders next day and had better have a good excuse.

Next morning I appeared before the Commandant, who was also the Assistant Chief Constable of the County I had joined. I told him that I had no excuse, that the others were not to blame and I was prepared to take the consequences. It had only been a joke to relieve the monotony of what had been a very dull morning. I got a real lecture on what being in charge meant and that if there was any more nonsense on my part I would not even complete the course. I left the office feeling about one inch tall.

There was no parade for meals in the strict sense, we all just walked in and sat down during the period set aside for meals. There was a cover over each meal and one day when the Commandant sat down he lifted his cover and then took off like a blue-arsed fly. His chair fell over and when he got up from the floor he had turned blue with rage. Underneath his cover was a grass snake! I knew there and then who had done this - it was a joker from a course ahead of me. We knew, but no one let on. He kept glaring at me and I honestly think he thought it was me. I didn't tell, neither did anyone else. The lads were learning what 'esprit de corps' meant.

One lad named M. who belonged to the Suffolk Constabulary, was kicked in the head while playing rugby. We thought after the game that there was something wrong with him. He didn't report sick but in class he suddenly fell over - he had got himself a fractured skull. He went to hospital and came back in a week, quite fit again.

Besides rugby we had all the other sports, football and hockey in particular, and one day I was called off the field while having a game of football, and a chap came and asked me if I would like a trial for Southampton Football Club. I declined the offer and was very surprised at it, but I had never heard that they were anything special, and besides I was thirty years of age and that was too old to start football as a professional. I had played in the army and never been picked for the Regimental team and there had been several men there far better than me. I wasn't good enough and wasn't going to take the chance. I thanked the chap for his offer though.

During my period at the school we had several cross-country runs, I didn't excel at these but just jogged along; there were no prizes for being first or third, so I just kept up with the rest and made sure I didn't come in last. One Friday we were informed that there would be a seven miles cros-country run in and around the area of Eynsham. The first ten would be granted a weekend, so I telephoned Clarice (by this time she knew where I was) and asked her if she could ring up her cousin who lived in the village of Woodstock to ask if we could stay, as I had the chance of a weekend off. She did this and to prove I could run

I came in second and got the weekend off. The Commandant didn't half give me a funny look when I came running in; he never could make me out, but years later, when he came back to our force, he congratulated me, stating that he knew then that I was on the way to being a good policeman. I was chuffed at this, and I have never let him down.

After three months my course was over and I reported to an east coast town. I was free of my mother and father-in-law - in fact if I'd gone any further I'd have been in the sea!

I was told to make my own way to my station and did so, via Oxford and London, catching a train at Liverpool Street to my station where I arrived at about 5 p.m. I was met at the station with a smiling greeting from a P.C. who later became a Detective Chief Inspector. He took me to a real good lodging for which I paid two pounds per week, all in. My new uniform was at my lodging, and next day this P.C. called for me and I was introduced to the other four men there and the Inspector; we had no Sergeant, but the Inspector was a real 'odd ball' of the old school.

On meeting the Inspector I was told that I could forget all I had learned at the training school, and I was pushed out on to the streets, a real rooky, more frightened of myself than the public. But I was determined to do a good job, and the very first morning on duty I had to deal with a minor road accident - very minor, some clot had run over a child's bike. I got over that, but the next was a real beauty. I saw an old chap drive up and park and I saw that his vehicle had no excise licence. Full of bizz I stopped him as he got out of his car and asked him about the licence. He said 'Do I have to have one?' I enlightened him on the subject and asked him his name which he gave as Colonel X, and having entered his name in my book he said 'Don't you know me?' I told him that I didn't know him from Adam and that he would be reported for the offence. He then said 'I sit on the bench', at which explanation I looked down the road towards the park benches. Talk about green, I was greener than one of Bird's Eye's Garden Peas. It turned out that he was Chairman of the Magistrates. When I put the report in I had a lecture from the Superintendant. 'You don't report Magistrates' I was told. But I had different ideas as I considered they were just the same as ordinary people and had to obey the law just the same. Suffice to say the Colonel was never brought to court. My friend in the Met., prior to my joining the Police Service, had informed me that magistrates were all either 'Deaf, dumb, daft or dopey'; I had met one of the latter. Seriously though, this is not always so.

I had arrived at my east coast town in June, the beginning of the summer season, and we were hard pushed to keep order in the town with lost kids, drunks and Yanks. The Inspector was a real card; many an hour was spent in the station at weekends while he told us how he had started his service. He could drink like a fish, and when he was merry he would start off at about 10 p.m. and go on so that we were lucky to get out of the station before midnight. He would tell us how his old Super was driven round the countryside by him in a pony and trap and how he would stop at at least one pub in every village and come home blotto. We used to have a good laugh, but the town suffered, for there were no police about, and there was always trouble which we had to clear up next day.

There wasn't much to patrol, a long seaside front of about half a mile, some hutments, a small town, numerous shops all making money out of the trippers and living off the fat when the season was over. The Inspector had been there for years. Everyone knew him and in the bars he drank free; he believed any old tale the inhabitants of the shops and stalls told him, especially if we had pulled them up for some minor offence or other. Villains called him by name, and really it was a Fred Carno's Army at our station. We didn't know where we were half the time; outstanding warrants were hidden up, and it was only after phone calls from our Super that they suddenly turned up and were executed. We got the blame, but we couldn't do much about it. The Inspector's brother-in-law was one of the Assistant Chief Constables and he could get away with blue murder. Arrests were few and far between; what arrests we did make the Inspector used to tell us to proceed by summons so that no history of the offenders was taken. The cells, you see, were under his house which was attached to the station, and his wife, he said, wasn't there to feed prisoners. It sounds fantastic, but that is how it was.

With four of us at the station or section office we worked so that two of us were on from 9 a.m. till 5 p.m. and in the evening 6 p.m. till 2 a.m.., the break of one hour was usuallycovered by the Inspector. We went home at 5 p.m. leaving him on the phone. This worked alright in

My colleagues in 1950

the winter, but in the summer we had to call in men from the surrounding country beats. These officers usually had anything from ten to twenty years service and were a great source of amusement telling us of happenings which were hard to believe, but true.

On one beat there was a man who had 'L' plates up and should have had a qualified driver with him. He had been fined once for driving unaccompanied, so this officer kept an eye on him. One night he saw this client driving along the road, and the qualified passenger seemed to be asleep, so the car was stopped. Well this man certainly didn't have a qualified driver. What he had done was drape his coat round his Labrador dog and set his trilby hat on its head, and the animal was sitting in the front passenger seat! Naturally this put a stop to this client's capers and he got a heavy fine.

Our station also had a big rural area to look after inland. There were about seven rural beats and we used to see all the men on a Friday, pay day, the meeting of the clans as it were. The majority had not been in the services, but there were about four of us who had, and we altered things I can tell you. The older men had had to report on their rest days where they were going and even to state where they could be found after duty. I can just imagine that taking place now! The wives certainly wouldn't have it, never mind the men.

The majority of us stuck together in all things; we helped each other and didn't tell tales, but we had a senior P.C. who thought he should supervise us lesser mortals. His wife was a friend of the Inspector's wife and anything the rest of us did always got back to the Inspector in one way or another. One day, one of the lads was off sick, He said he had tonsilitis and I really think he had. He had a doctor's certificate confirming the fact, but our Inspector didn't believe it, so while we were in the station receiving our orders he mentioned that he was going to see that 'joker' who was sick and catch him out. He thought he was malingering. Anyway, I was out first from the station and got round to this lad's lodging and told him what had been said; malingering or not I wasn't going to see him get caught. We were mates and stuck together. Someone told the Inspector he had seen me coming from the area of the P.C. who was sick and about three days later I was called before the Inspector and got a real telling off. I was told that I was still on probation and I'd better mind my P s and Q s and not tell anyone that he was going to be visited on speck.

Each day we had not only to make our pocket books up but also make a report in a journal of what we had done that day. It was a hard job to really put down everything, but after I had seen what the older P.C.s put down I was soon able to cut it all down to a minute phrase of 'Office duty and patrol'. Then at the end of the month we had to write it all down on a huge sheet called a 'Monthly Return'; all 'crime messages' had to go into it and 'express messages' about murders etc. went in red. The day I was on office duty and found I had my journal to do and 'Monthly Return' there was no red ink, not a drop; the only thing available was a red crayon pencil, so I sharpened this up and did the job that way, it looked O.K. and I couldn't see anything wrong with it, neither could anyone else, but the Inspector's friend saw it and he reported me. Another telling off! I took no notice, but it was very disconcerting to have this person always telling tales.

At that time all 'Found Property' was handed in at our station. Sometimes a slip was given so that it could be claimed after three months by the finder, but our Inspector would talk the finder out of having a receipt. Anything valuable went this way, and was sold by our Inspector. A good camera had been handed in like that, and was sold to our P.C. It did him some good, for we had a raid on a brothel and he took the photos with it. As a result he was seconded to the C.I.D. and never looked back.

There was one man in the town who had our Inspector's number. He worked at the Post Office and knew our friend through and through. He held a bit of sway in the town. I was on patrol in the High Street and this man came out of the Post Office and asked what was being done about all the shop doorways and windows that had been daubed with yellow paint advising people to vote for a certain Party (it wasn't Labour, I can tell you). I told him other than inspect the damage I had no idea. I was told to get the Inspector and tell him that if he didn't find out who had done the daubing, he would be reported to the committee. Well I did just what I had been requested, and you never saw such a change in a man when I told him. He didn't say a word, shot out of the office like a blue bottle and the next thing I saw, later in the day, was a gang of the 'upper crust' of the town scraping and cleaning the mess away. There certainly were no reports put in.

Being both rural and urban we had a variety jobs to do. Once I went with a senior P.C. to an outlying seaside village where a man had committed suicide by shooting himself through the mouth. He had lived with his brother. We called a doctor to pronounce the victim dead, then, having got the body away, we were helping the brother to clean up the mess, when he said 'Would you like some honey?' We thought we were being given it, but on handing the jars of honey to us he said 'That'll be five shillings.' He soon knew what we thought of him. That was my first 'sudden death', one of many.

One death I attended caused a real commotion. The poor old chap died outside a public house, right on the main road. I got there to deal with the matter and found an elderly gentleman sitting up, eyes wide open and looking ahead as if he were watching the traffic. A nice old lady sat by him and, not seeing or thinking the old chap was dead, I asked the old lady if she had seen anything of a sudden death in the area. She began to cry; the old chap still sat there with his hands on his lap and, amid tears, she said 'It's him' pointing to the man. He was dead alright and it gave me quite a turn. I called a doctor who certified death. The licensee didn't want the body in the pub, so I put him over my shoulder and took him upstairs into a store room and laid him there, but when we came to remove him, the coffin wouldn't go up the stairs. So we got a block and tackle and hauled the coffin up through the window then lowered him down the same way. Lesson one regarding where to put bodies was learned by me that day.

I had to deal one day with a most tragic accident. A little boy had come with his parents to the seaside, He had been put into the swimming pool about 10 a.m. and the parents had gone off on their own. At about 9 p.m. they came reporting that their young lad, a child of about nine years of age, was missing. From the description given he answered to that of a little lad who at about 7 p.m. had been pulled out of the swimming pool, dead. It appeared that he must have dived in, hit his head on the bottom and been under water from then on, with hundreds of swimmers passing over him and not noticing. It was really distressing. I couldn't understand why the parents hadn't gone to the pool during the day to see how the little lad was getting on, but I didn't voice any opinion, their loss being so terrible.

One night, our Inspector came in from a different area from the one which he usually haunted. He told me that someone had reported a load of mines behind a wall on a coastal village main road. I deduced where it was and cycled to the scene about four miles away. I found the mines - pressure mines, that I had dealt with during the war. These had been left behind when the army evacuated the area and forgotten. On the way back, after putting some red lights in the area, I came across a bright lad, a house-breaker whom I recognised, and took him to our station and, without telling the Inspector, locked him in one of our cells. He wasn't going to break in in our town. I telephoned the army at Colchester to remove the mines - they were all on 'Secure' so were safe enough to handle, about ten of them - and after this I went home to my lodging and very early in the morning I got the chap from the cells and escorted him from the town. I certainly didn't tell the Inspector what I had done. I had applied the 'Ways and Means Act'.

That summer we had a lot of thefts from the beach and we wanted someone to try and stop this type of crime. So they sent down to us a Detective Constable from H.Q., and he walked along amongst the bathers wearing a trilby hat and a blue suit. He had about as much chance of lifting a thief dressed like that as of flying. We had had a W.P.C. sent to us for the summer, but no one thought of employing her and a P.C. on the beach, dressed like everyone else. Needless to say there was no arrest made.

One Sunday morning along with another officer I was patrolling along the promenade when I looked over and saw the dead body of an elderly gentleman. There weren't any people about and after we had had the doctor pronounce him dead I called the C.I.D. as there were no means of identification on the body or clothing. The pockets of the suit the man wore were filled with sand, there were no injuries to the body either, so it appeared that it was a clear case of suicide, which it turned out later it was. In the meanwhile, using a gasworks hut as a mortuary we had our C.I.D. officer come along both for fingerprinting and photos. I know it was a serious business, but we couldn't help laughing, for we had to sit the body up and bob down while it was photographed. Well it kept falling over, and our D.C. kept saying to the corpse 'A fat lot of co-operation I'm getting from you!' It took about an hour to get that job done, and then the fingerprinting took place. By then rigor mortis had set in and the fingers were stiff and tight together. The printing should be done by rolling the paper on the fingers, but not our D.C. He kept trying to roll the fingers which was next to impossible, and moaning all the time about non-cooperation from the corpse. Poor old boy; we found later, when his home was searched and a letter found, that he was a retired schoolmaster and was about to re-marry. His grown-up children didn't agree to this as he was well off and they thought they would lose out in his will.

During my first tour of duty at this station I learned quickly. It was good training, but it could have been better if we'd had a good senior officer. Our Clerk Sergeant used to say 'That Inspector will disillusion any young officer', but he didn't disillusion me.

One night there were a number of T.A. Royal Artillery soldiers in the town, and I came across three of them at about midnight looking for lodgings. They appeared to be very well-conducted and happy; they had had a few drinks but were just merry, no trouble at all. I found them a very good place for the night at one of the minor Guest Houses. The lady had a son of her own in the army and she knew I was also an ex-soldier. They had no money, so while I was there they tipped out their respective pay books as means of identity; I took particulars and went on my way. I entered the facts in the O.B. and blow me, some sneak informed the Inspector of what I had done. I was called 'wet' for the soldiers would certainly never pay. I didn't like this and told both Inspector and P.C. that all soldiers weren't like that. This didn't go down well, and I thought there goes another black mark. I was as pleased as punch when I was called to the Guest House and shown a letter and a thirty shillings Postal Order which had been sent by the soldiers. I took it to the station and took great delight in showing both P.C. and Inspector, but all I got from them was that they were exceptions. I like trusting people until it is proved to the contrary. It has never failed.

One day I was sent to a village on the main coast road to direct several army tanks through the village. I was getting on O.K. and the tanks were rumbling through when an elderly man of about sixty years came up in front of me and kept dancing about telling me he had a son in the police force. I thought he must be a lunatic and grabbed him by the seat of the pants and set him on the pavement. He told me he was going to report me, but I heard no more about the matter.

⊰※⊱

Summer being over, I was posted. I had been down to see my wife and son, but she hadn't wanted to travel that year with the baby. That was fair and I didn't blame her, but where I got sent to was one of the worst beats possible, right out in the country. My lodgings were not bad, they were terrible! - so much so that I was ill, and was posted back to where I had come from. But not before we went through a real ordeal, myself, my little son and my wife. I was stationed with an older P.C. and he was the best I have ever been with; he is dead now, but he was a real good sort. We also had an Inspector there, who had more cars during the four months I was there than I had hot dinners at my new lodging. Still that was incidental; he never hurt me.

My new lodging now was nearly as bad as the last. It was almost outside the village at the home of the widow of a blacksmith. She had a son of nineteen and when I was sent there I found that I had to sleep in the same room as the lad, not only that but my bed had only two blankets and sheets on it and one pillow. I had to use my greatcoat as a blanket it was so cold, there not being any type of heating in the room.

For breakfast I had porridge and a piece of toast. I was told it was two slices of toast and no porridge or one slice with. I had it *with*. At lunch I got cold meat every day plus parsnips (which I hate) and boiled potatoes. There was no sweet, and at tea there was bread and butter plus a part of a tea-cake, and at night dry bread and cheese plus a mug of cocoa. What a diet! I was starved, never any greens, so that when I was out on patrol I was always glad when invited into a house or other to have a cup of tea and a biscuit.

There was very little to do on this beat, plenty of fields and woods and three churches. I spent more time in the churches than anywhere else in the hope of catching an offertory box-breaker, but I didn't - not there.

To pass the time the older P.C. and I used to go and get out law books and he would take the place of an offender and show me how to deal with all sorts of matters from aliens to firearm certificates and more serious crimes. He was a really good instructor, so much so that I passed my Constable – Sergeant's Exam first go.

One thing that took place when I was out in the wilds was that the Inspector told me that I could look at any book, in any drawer and do what I liked in the office. We had to make the fire each day and every Monday clear the office, for this was also the local courtroom, believe it or not (now defunct). The cleaning of the station took a couple of hours and the elder P.C. and I had our hands full dealing with callers on any manner of things, especially Pig or Animal Movement licences, for not only were we P.Cs. for the County but Animal Inspectors as well.

Well one night I was alone in the office about 10 p.m., and after rummaging through a drawer I found a Colt Automatic Pistol. I thought I had unloaded it for I took the butt magazine out and saw that it was full of bullets. I was looking at the weapon and at the same time I squeezed the trigger, there was the most awful bang and a bullet whipped past my head and straight into the wall. I had a fright I can tell you. The older P.C., who lived next door to the station, came running in and saw me as white as a sheet. I told him what had taken place, and we saw there was a dirty big hole in the wall, so we got some filler from his house and renovated the wall, taking out the flattened bullet. We didn't tell anyone and the Inspector knew nothing of the matter.

Coupled with the station duty in this outlandish spot, we had to make a 'point' (place to be met); no one was ever there to mark our pocket books but the 'points' were in the most outlandish places, miles from nowhere. If I'd seen a rabbit it would have been company. One 'point' was at least five miles from the station, always at 11 p.m., and we had to stop there for a quarter of an hour *in case*. In case of what? After the point we had some three quarters of an hour to get back and sign off. Still, I liked the country, but it turned out that my wife didn't, and this is where things went radically wrong over the years.

I didn't stay very long at this station for two things took place which altered my life. One was that I got a perforated ulcer. I was giving evidence at court and prior to going into the witness box I felt really bad. My stomach hurt so much that I ran down to the pub close by the court and asked for and drank a double whiskey. Then, when I came to give evidence in a case of cattle-rustling, I collapsed. It was a good job there was a doctor in court at the time - I had a burst ulcer and peritonitis had set in. I was whipped off to hospital right away and operated on immediately. The doctor's being in the court saved my life. But worse was to come. I got a telephone message sent to the hospital regarding my infant son. He was just two then, and he had been rushed to hospital, to Great Ormond Street, London. I was released from hospital myself on the 20th December 1948 and went immediately to my wife's home. They had had the child ill for a week or so before calling the doctor in and when the doctor saw him he was so shocked that he ordered the ambulance at once. I had only been informed of the telephone message sent by my wife on the day I left hospital; I was not told of it before because of my condition, so that in all I had been from 1st to the 20th December 1948 in ignorance of the fate of my child. The fault lay not on the part of the hospital but of my father-in-law. He didn't believe in doctors and wouldn't let my wife call anyone till it was almost too late. I didn't half tell him off when I got down there.

My infant son appeared to recover so that by about 6th January 1949 he was discharged from hospital, but I was told that he had leukaemia, at least it was suspected, and, if it were so, he would die that year. It really upset me, but fate was fate. My wife didn't bat an eyelid, but she turned grey almost overnight. She was then thirty-one years of age. She didn't show her sorrow outwardly at all but kept it pent up inside.

Being on 'sick leave' I had very little money, in fact I was almost broke. What we had, we needed to live on and it looked as if we were in for a really bleak Christmas. The lads from my old Section sent me ten pounds which was most gratefully received and appreciated. I decided we wouldn't go to see little Brian on Christmas Day as perhaps he would have cried on our leaving him; we went instead on Boxing Day and he looked a picture and full of life. He didn't look ill at all - little did we know what was to come.

On my son being released from hospital I went back to my country beat, but I told the Inspector I was not going back to my old billet and that if my lodging wasn't altered I would report the matter, and those responsible for picking this lodging. I had hardly got this off my chest before I was transferred back to my old beat by the sea.

Chapter 11. Beside the Seaside

Being posted back to the seaside town was a godsend. The Americans had come back to their old bases in Norfolk, and didn't they liven things up! We had some of them at our station and one, a Master Sergeant Cornelius, from Dallas, Texas, was a real racist. He hated the blacks, and, being a Military Policeman, he vented his spleen on them for the slightest infringement of the regulations, like having a button undone or not wearing their hats; our cells were always full up with them till about two o'clock in the morning.

I had a fat argument with this Sergeant one night about rationing. I told him that it meant everyone had a fair chance to get food, especially sugar and butter, but he wouldn't have that and when I said it really meant fair shares for all he said 'You're a Communist'. I told him in no uncertain terms where he got off. He also said that when they were in charge they would ban bicycles from the roads. I let fly at this, 'In charge! Not as long as you have a hole in your backside will that happen - you've a shock coming if you think it will'. He was dumbfounded and said he couldn't understand us. To cut a long story short, I enlightened him on a few things about the Americans at war and he never argued with me again, ever.

During the winter, if it had not been for the Americans taking over at one of our big bases, the town would have been dead; we would have been lucky if we had seen a seagull on the beach. One thing it did for us was that we could now at least arrest people and put them in the cells. Mostly they were American servicemen in any case and with their own 'Snowballs', as they called the Military Police, it meant that prisoners could be looked after without any effort on the part of the Inspector.

In all, the Americans brought a breath of fresh air into the town and plenty of money flowed over the bars, but there were numerous fights, especially over girls, and we had an influx of prostitutes as you can well imagine. They could be picked out as easy as pie, for, not being local, they stood out like sore thumbs.

We raided a couple of brothels that had begun to operate in the town and raided a well known hotel. Mr Quintin Hogg, later to become Lord Hailsham and Lord Chancellor defended. He lost, but it was not for want of trying on his part. During the court proceedings Mr Hogg brought in a tremendous number of books and papers tied with pink ribbon. I believe it was brought into court to try and intimidate the local magistrates, but it had no effect on our Chairman for he was a K.C. in his own right. The rolls all tied up were actually conveyance notices, nothing to do with the case. I know for I had a look while everyone was away at lunch.

The reign of our Inspector was coming to an end. The Assistant Chief Constable, the one who had been our Commandant at the Training School, was now back with the Force. He was over most weekends; he didn't come to the station but used to walk round the town and then clear off. The writing was on the wall.

One day, along with another officer whom I shall call John, I was called to an old fisherman's cottage at the old part of the town. It was alleged that an old lady lived there and she hadn't been seen for days. There was a council workman living there, but this man was totally indifferent to what was happening to the old lady. On getting to the address we had been given, we had to force open the front door; there was no rear door or window. The sight that greeted us is beyond description - we could have been entering a home of some four hundred years before. There was a table in the centre of a room some eight feet by twelve feet; it was covered in filth and dirty cups, plates, jam jars, candles and crusts of bread and bits of meat, it was awful. There were only two chairs and they were both broken and backless, while around the walls of the room were cinders and refuse about two feet out into the room and about two feet high. We had to push the door hard, for behind it we found a little wizened old lady. She had red bite-marks all over her face, and she appeared to be dead, but in fact was unconscious as we found out. There were rat holes all about the cinders and it was plain to see that we had arrived just in time - she was literally being eaten alive. Calling an ambulance, we had her sent to the hospital, but as soon as she was undressed and put in a bath, poor dear, she died.

Having got the old lady to hospital we sent for a Welfare Officer and began a systematic search of the place. You see we had found one gold sovereign on the floor. We didn't have any special suits in those days, so we took off our jackets and began to sift the cinders and search the place. It took all day and we found approximately three hundred gold sovereigns in the mess, on the table, on the floor, under the table and in the cinders and ashes. Upstairs, for there were only two rooms to this cottage, we found only one bed. It was wet with urine, and there was a great hole in the mattress. There was also male clothing here and from that we realised that this council workman had been living upstairs. Where the old lady had slept I couldn't tell you. I guess she kept her clothes on and slept on one of the chairs downstairs. She must have been about ninety years of age.

The upshot of the affair was that we had to hand the money found to our Inspector. Long before the inquest he had handed it over to a relative he found. Nothing was said at the inquest, but it made us think, for it appeared that there were numerous relatives in the new town, none of whom had ever come forward to help her, but once she was dead they were like flies round a jam pot. In the course of time the recipient of the money opened a shop near the sea-front and did very well. Such is life.

Then came the time when we got rid of our Inspector. There was to be a raid on a big guest house. Several men had been brought in from the surrounding beats and it was planned for about 11 p.m. on a Sunday night. I was left in charge of the station and that night, when the officers had gone, led by our Superintendant, the Inspector came in and told me to put the phone switch over to his house. I did this, then a couple of minutes later it was switched back to me.

I thought the raid would take an hour or so, but in reality it took about half an hour and that was counting the journey there on foot which was about a quarter of a mile from the station. The Superintendant came charging in to the station, livid with rage, and asked me if I had used the phone. I told him I had not, and he kept saying 'You sure?' and 'You'll bloody well regret it if I find you did use it'. I told him I was not a liar, but seeing that I was likely to be made the scapegoat I informed him that as soon as he had left the station with the men, the Inspector had had the phone transferred to him for a minute or so and that he might have made a call. The Super went blind with rage, charged into the Inspector's house and slammed the door. I don't know what went on in there but next day the Assistant Chief Constable called at the station. I was again on duty there and he told me to clear off for an hour which I did. When I returned, the Inspector had gone indoors, so what went on I don't know, but it was something serious, for next day we learned that the Inspector had put in his resignation and was leaving at the end of the month; we were really glad.

It would appear that as the raid was about to take place, about forty or so men ran out of this guest house; some even came out of the windows as the raiding party entered the grounds. From one of these men who had got out of the window it was gleaned that a phone call had been received and as the result they had all been warned to clear the premises. This was the raid that went wrong; it was talked about for months.

Except for myself, the whole station, the five others who were there with me, were all sent to different stations in the county. One lad, who had had enough, resigned and went to Canada and became a sheriff. he wrote and told us that we should come out there for there were jobs for good police officers, but no one did. Only one stayed in the area, the up and coming C.I.D. man. He really made good, cured of his ways, and I began to get on with him; he became a real friend.

During the next few months I passed my Inspector's Exam., but it didn't do me any good at all for I fell foul of our Super in the following way. I had about four years service in by now and was really feeling my feet, then one day there appeared on Divisional Orders that all Probationer Constables would have to attend Div.H.Q. once a month for Discussion Classes. The order said these officers would attend in police time, but those not on Probation would do so in their own time. This included myself and one other, plus a lad who had just transferred from the Met. It was also stated that if this day fell on our rest day we could also attend, but if not attending should put in a report stating the reasons why we were not availing ourselves of the opportunity. I took exception to this, for on a rest day it was my business what I did. Another officer thought the same and we decided that we would not put in a report. Well, came pay day and the Super had us all in the office. He began by letting several go except the new Met. lad, myself and John. He then got on to telling us what he thought of us in general. The Met. lad hadn't put a report in because he was not at the station when we had got the Div. Order, so he was in the clear. It was John and I who got the brunt of the Super's attack. He was beginning to swear at us when suddenly the Met. lad stopped him saying, 'There's no reason for you to use language like that Sir'. The Super nearly took off, he choked back what he intended saying and began again in a quieter tone starting with me. 'Troup, you're a Bolshie,' he said, 'you don't know what esprit de corps is'. I couldn't believe my ears and told him that I had served twelve years in the Norfolk Regiment, all the war included, and that esprit de corps was the beginning and end of all comradeship in the army. I let rip, and told him that I had been all over the world during the war. I honestly thought I had gone too far, but instead he took it, and then he looked up and said 'I'll tell you what Troup, you'll never be promoted while you're in this Constabulary', to which I replied 'Can I note that in my pocket book sir?' At this he jumped up and left the station, both he and I had gone too far. I did note what he had said in my pocket book and the young Met. lad signed his name below. I never did get promoted! The young lad has been a friend to me over the years; he is a lay preacher and practices what he preaches. He has told me off for swearing at times; I try to keep it down when he is around, honouring his way of life.

I never was promoted, for in the Force records are kept of a man's service; there is one record that you can see, but there is another one that no one sees, and this is the one that 'cooks your goose'. Many a man has not been promoted through this type of record.

One day I was on duty at the church to be attended by the King. We just had to see that no one interfered with the progress of the royal party. I was told that I would be on the iron gate which led directly from the house to the church. I was to undo the gate, let the royal party through, not salute, nor speak to the King - I couldn't see what he would want to speak to me for anyway. All went well and I did as I was told. Usually the church service lasted for one full hour to the dot. Well this Sunday it didn't. While the royal party was at their worship, I was told to take a break and get back in time for the return of the family. Off I went and sat in our patrol car outside the gate. Half an hour passed and then there was a great rushing to and fro. I went to have a look; the royal party was half way from the church to the iron gate! If I had been Jesse Owens I couldn't have got to the gate in time; all I saw was the Superintendant, gamp under his arm, one hand holding his bowler hat, tearing along like mad to get to the gate before the King. Luckily for me, although the royal party had to stop, I had left the key to the gate in the lock, otherwise he would have had to walk home. Meanwhile I turned tail and, arriving at the patrol car, told the driver we were dismissed. He didn't believe me at first, but I convinced him. This was a lie I had told him, but off we went back to my Section Office and meal break. That was not the end of the affair as you can well imagine.

At about 2.30 p.m. I had a call from the Super. He asked for me, and when I informed him it was Troup speaking he started up, 'Are you on patrol this afternoon?' I informed him I was. He then said 'Do you go near the pier?' Again I informed him that I did, to which he said 'Is the tide in?' I replied that I didn't know but would find out and tell him if he wanted me to. To this reply I got 'I'm not interested in the tide you bloody fool, whether it's in or out is of little matter. If it's in, all the better, you can go to the end of the pier and jump off!' When this was said he slammed the phone down. I think he wasn't too pleased over the way I had looked after the gate for the King. It was just after this incident that the King died, I hope he didn't blame me for it. Such is life, trouble is half of my name.

When King George VI died it meant extra duties, but I was O.K. for I was left in charge of the station. The number of Americans who called and wanted to know how they could get to see the coffin was considerable; they appeared to be taking it all like a joy ride, but I told them I had no information and left it at that.

At the time of the death we had the B.B.C. chief commentator come down with his crew. The night I must tell you of, he was lording it in the local pub surrounded by several cronies, while the locals stood there with their tongues hanging out listening to him. I had to go in and get him, for the big radio van was outside with its doors open and every Tom, Dick and Harry, including Americans, getting in and looking round. He was a good commentator but as for security he hadn't a clue. I didn't want anything stolen from the van, so I informed his nibs what was going on. He took not the slightest bit of notice at first till I really set about him, then he got outside and sent for some of his crew. The van was then moved and locked. He thanked me later as things would have been pretty sticky for him if some of the radio equipment had been stolen. It was the attitude of the man that got me, he was the great 'I am' and how dare I speak to him. Mind you he was extremely good at his job and deserved the credit he got for that.

One time we had a political meeting at what was known as the Town Hall, a sad little building near the sea front; it was used more as an auctioneer's hall than a Town Hall, but that was what it was called, and along with another P.C. my Met. friend, we found a vehicle parked in darkness right across the road. It hadn't been there long but it was a real danger, and being black could hardly be seen on a dark misty night. We made enquiries and found that the vehicle belonged to Lady ...., a J.P. Her excuse was that she wanted to hear the speaker at the meeting, so I reported her for the offence. Well you would have thought I had committed an offence against *her*, for after my report got to the Superintendant he came to the station and told me that J.Ps weren't reported (as if I didn't know) but the offence was committed and I did report the woman. Why not? Anyone else would have been 'done' as the saying is.

⎯⫛⎯

During all this time I was on the look-out for a place for my wife and little Brian. They came down for a holiday and had a good month at the seaside, but it wasn't till they had gone back that I found a place. It was part-furnished but was only about two pounds per week, so I rang Clarice up and told her to be ready on the Saturday with the Bank Book and we would go to the Post Office, draw our money out and get some really good furniture. On the Saturday I managed to get a lorry, ten pounds for the round trip, and off we went early in the morning, arriving at about twelve noon at Teddington. I waited while we had a meal and then asked Clarice for the Bank Book. She didn't give it to me at first and hummed and ha-ed over the matter. We were seated at lunch at the time, she sitting right in front of me beside her father. I got a bit upset with her evasive attitude, till at last I told her to get the book. What a shock I had! We should have had over four hundred pounds, but when I looked through the book I found we had the princely sum of three shillings and threepence halfpenny. She had spent the lot! I was so wild I jumped up and slapped her across the face. Her father didn't like it nor did her mother - those blighters had been milking her dry, and what with her going out with her cousin, the money had gone.

What a start to our new home! Still, we packed up what we had and left for my new place. I think it was from here that everything went wrong with my marriage, but exactly one month to the day after this I had a terrible shock. I was on nights and decided at about 4 a.m. to call at my home for a cup of tea. I looked into the bedroom. Little Brian sat up and blood shot out of his nose and mouth. I woke my wife and ran to a telephone and had the doctor call. The place was like a slaughter-house, blood everywhere. The upshot was that Brian's nose was plugged and by 6.30 a.m., uniform and all, I was off to London on the train arriving at Liverpool Street Station at 10 a.m. The taxi driver who took me to Great Ormond Street refused payment for the ride from Liverpool Street, and as soon as Brian was examined he was whipped away to a ward. I stayed all day, then, leaving my wife in London, I went back to my Section Office. I told what had taken place but wasn't granted any leave, so it was 2 p.m. two days later when I was again at Great Ormond Street. I was informed that Brian had got leukaemia and that he was dying. There was no hope and he wouldn't last the day. Clarice sat by his side holding his little hand. She didn't cry - it would have been better if she had. The little mite, who was only two years nine months old, kept asking her for a cup of tea and an Irish nurse kept telling him to be quiet. We were in a cubicle separated from the other children so he was not disturbing anybody, so in the end I told her Brian was going to be quiet for all eternity, and she could shut up. At 3 p.m. precisely he died, calling for his mum with his last breath, and then a funny thing took place, a little sparrow flew in the window, settled on the bed and then flew off. Cry, I cried from then until he was buried. I got a week's leave for this. He was buried near a children's playground at Teddington Cemetery. There I left him; I have never been back to his little grave. The reason for this will be told later.

I didn't speak of my son's death for years, not till one day I met an old chap whose son had died like mine some forty years earlier. It was then I realised that I was not the only one in the world to have tragedy strike them. My wife never said a word; her hair went snow white from grey. We had two more sons later, within three years of each other, but she never got over Brian, of that I am certain now.

⇒✦⇐

On the beat

It was O.K. being in furnished rooms; it was cheap and clean, and we managed to put a bit of money by. Being in a good job, I was satisfied; Clarice wasn't. She didn't like the town, she didn't like the people and worst of all she didn't like me being in the Police Service. She wanted to go back to Teddington and her family. We rowed and made up time out of number, but it was no use. Eventually I got a council house, and I got it through the back door in a way. This is how.

I knew almost everyone in town and they knew me. There were a few council houses being built in the old town, and I made enquiries but was told 'no chance'. I left it at that till all the houses were built and fit for occupation, and then I asked who had No.1. I was told that a certain party had been allocated this house. I nearly had a fit, for this man was part-owner of a hotel, not a big one, but one that brought in a good bit of cash and had about twenty to thirty guests all summer. On learning this, I went to the Clerk of the Council and told him what I had learned. He admitted that it was true, so I asked 'What about chaps like me?' He told me he would find out. Well lo and behold, two days later I was allocated a house. I didn't tell anyone else, but that was how I got my first house.

Our new Inspector was a bit of a disciplinarian, but a good sort; if we did our job he didn't complain, and he kept us on our toes.

One day we had a complaint from a lady in a part of the town which overlooked the sea. She said a man was believed to be firing a gun near her house and bullets had hit her fence, so I said I would deal with the matter. I informed the Inspector and told him I believed it must be a .22 and I would confiscate the gun, for there was no one in that area who had a firearms certificate for a .22 weapon. 'Now how do you hope to seize the weapon?' said he. I told him I would think about the matter on the way to the man's home. (In those days we did gun licence enquiries for the Council, for anyone having a licensed gun last year, and who didn't renew the licence this year, was the subject of an enquiry). Anyway I got to the house and found that the man was a Pole. I asked him for his gun licence and he informed me that he didn't have one, but now that I had called, he would get one. I then got chatting to him and asked him to show me the weapon. I could not seize a shotgun then, but I could a firearm like a .22. He brought the weapon, and it was indeed a .22 which I took from him, learned who he had bought it from and both were brought to court for the offences disclosed. I had done this just to show the Inspector that there was more than one way to skin a rabbit, as the saying goes.

During the time I was in this section with our new Inspector I again got ulcers and it took me all my time to crawl round my beat. One night I was on patrol near to the sea front at about 8 p.m. on a Sunday night. The tide was in and there were literally thousands milling around the bars nearby, including several American servicemen. They weren't doing any harm and the crowds were out for a good time. In fact it was a typical day's end at the seaside until a woman of about thirty years of age came up while I was speaking to one of the 'Snowballs' and said 'I've been raped'. I nearly fell down, for her appearance didn't match her story. She was smartly dressed and showed no sign of anything which would point out to me that her allegation was true. She then said 'That's him over there,' pointing to an American serviceman who was then entering a bar. The 'Snowball' who was with me was going to arrest the man there and then but I restrained him and asked him if he knew the man; he did and also the unit he belonged to. I then told him that I would question the woman further and took her to the Police Station. There was no senior officer to be found so I set about questioning the woman on my own.

I asked her when the alleged rape had taken place, and she said 'Last Thursday night'. I was instantly suspicious, for rape victims if they are going to report the matter, do so as soon as possible, either to a friend or to a police officer. Noting all she was saying I then asked her how she had come into contact with the soldier she had alleged raped her. She informed me that she had met him in a certain bar in the town and that after a few drinks she had agreed to go for a ride with him in his car. Getting out of the town they had gone to an area which was partially wooded and had long grass near some tall trees, they'd gone over to this spot, the American had held her arm tightly and carried a blanket with him, he'd put the blanket down on the ground still holding her, believe it or not, she alleged she just couldn't get away, besides it was still light at the time and the area was quite close to the main road. It all sounded very far-fetched to me, he was then alleged to have taken her knickers down and done the job. I asked her if she had had her clothing torn and she told me that nothing like that had taken place. I then told her that I didn't believe her and I wanted to know the truth. Well out it came. Yes, she had had sexual intercourse with the serviceman, that was true, but he hadn't forced her in any way. The fact was that she was a divorcee and she said that if she had had a child by this man she would lose her alimony from her ex-husband. This was the truth of it.

I then got this all down in statement form; it had taken about three hours to get it all out of her. There had been no policewoman to depend on and my ulcer was really playing me up. I got hold of the American officer in charge of the 'Snowballs' that night and told him that he could forget about making any arrest - the allegation was false. There was nothing we could do about it, for this was in the days before 'wasting police time' had become an offence.

Later that night one of the P.C.s who had been on patrol in the area of the alleged rape reported to me that he had seen the incident and far from the American holding the girl, she had run into the field and helped him lay the blanket down. I got the report next day and sent it in, but I was now so ill that I was taken to hospital where I was operated on and spent the next three weeks in bed.

When I got out of hospital I had two more weeks off and then was back on duty. The affair of the woman who had made the allegation of rape was all cleared up. I met the soldier concerned and he was really pleased. Thank goodness, he said, that it had not taken place in America, it would have taken months to clear up.

One night I had to go to a fire. The Inspector thought it only a tiny one, but in fact the old hall in the old part of the town was on fire and it gutted the lot. We had six engines there. The roof appeared to be alight first; the place had been turned into flats and it was full of American families and did I have a job getting them out of bed? They didn't believe me at first, but the smell of the smoke soon woke them up. We cleared as much of their belongings as we could from the rooms. At the height of the blaze a cat was on the roof top running along the ledge; parts of the roof were falling in and some nut was getting a ladder to get up and rescue it. I stopped him and told him that if there was to be a hero it would be me and just as I said this the complete roof fell in. The leaded windows of the building all melted and every bit of wood was burnt up. I got away from the area at about 10 a.m. the next day. The Inspector wanted to know why I was late coming on duty and when I told him I was just reporting 'off duty' he had a fit and asked why I hadn't informed him. The phones had all been burnt up, that was why. Anyway the upshot was that I got a Chief Constable's Commendation for the fire and my report.

I seemed to be always dealing with American servicemen, for there were now thousands visiting our little town. We had our hands full dealing with them and if it hadn't been for the 'Snowballs' we would have been unable to cope.

One day I received a report of a suspicious person near some chicken runs on the outskirts of the town. I went to investigate. To get to the scene where these chicken runs were, I had to go down a cinder track bounded by a ploughed field on my left and a thick hedge on my right. I rode my cycle along the path; it was a lovely summer's day I remember, and I was not paying particular attention to anything when suddenly I hit the deck. A person in khaki uniform, dirty and unkempt and dressed like an American serviceman had sprung out of the hedge and run off across the ploughed field. My dignity was upset to say the least, but I wasn't fool enough to go chasing over the ploughed field after him, so I picked up my cycle and rode round the field and watched him cross the main road and make towards the sea. I followed and eventually cornered him near some old buildings.

By this time there were several people about, I should think in the region of fifty or so, and as I advanced towards him he pulled a great long knife from his boot. It seemed like a sword to me. I stopped full in my tracks, then drew my truncheon and advanced. He then got the knife by its tip and swung his arm back to throw it. I threw my truncheon at him and missed. My heart skipped a beat. I called to someone to ring the Police Station and tell them where I was and that I needed assistance (didn't I just?). I kept advancing on the man, talking to him and telling him not to be a fool and kept this up for about five minutes (at the time it seemed like hours) when suddenly I saw our senior P.C coming towards me and behind the man, riding his cycle. The soldier didn't hear him coming and the front wheel of the cycle caught him right up the backside. By now I was so close I kicked him hard in front and jumped on him, grabbed the knife, turned him over and handcuffed him. There was loud applause from the people gathered round. In getting hold of the knife I cut my hand slightly and the blood was everywhere.

When the Superintendent learned what had taken place he told me that I would be on a Misconduct Report for not using the correct police hold in arresting this soldier who turned out to be an escapee from the stockade at the local Air Base. But when the Chief Constable came over, he congratulated me and asked how my cut hand was. I got another Commendation from him, much to the chagrin of our Superintendant.

One night I was standing on the other side of the road to one of our pubs. It was choc-a-bloc with American servicemen who on the whole were well behaved. Never mind about what they got up to with the girls, it was no worse or better than we did when we were abroad. Anyway, suddenly the window to the pub shot up and the licensee was bawling to me to help. There were about thirty or more servicemen in the main bar, but they were all in a semi-circle facing one of our locals who was offering to fight the lot - he was drunk and fighting mad. So in I went to get this man out, grabbed him by one arm and was lucky in that the door was open and that the stairs were clear. I threw him down the stairs and pushed him out of the front door. He then went to re-enter the premises so I decided to arrest him, and that was when the real fun began. I got him on to the road just as our patrol car was passing. The vehicle stopped. The driver didn't get out but the observer who was with him got into the back seat ready to receive my prisoner. Well I got the back door of the vehicle open, but every time I went to push my prisoner in he put his foot on the step. Try as I might he wouldn't get in. With this going on I had my hands full when suddenly I received a great wallop to my head. The prisoner's girl friend had come out of the pub and began to batter me with her handbag. What with trying to get my drunk into the car, and fend her off, I let go of him at which he turned and aimed a haymaker at me. I ducked and gave him one right round the earhole, but in ducking I also heard a thump and then someone fell to the floor. I looked down and there was our lone Policewoman (she had been drafted in after the rape affair) flat on her back - she was out for the count. I then walloped the prisoner good and hard and he lay back, dead to the world in the patrol car where he was handcuffed. The policewoman fortunately revived and dealt with the woman and we took them both up to the station where they were charged with the offences committed.

Next morning I saw what I had done to the prisoner; he was a gory mess. The girl was O.K. and so was the policewoman, but when we took them to court both were fined two pounds for the assault on me and the policewoman, and ten shillings for being drunk and disorderly. Well, that was justice alright.

One thing that came out of this was that the prisoner always came to see me when he came into town. He became a real good sort and if I seemed likely to get into trouble, I always found him nearby, ready to give assistance.

I think this was the only time that the Super really thanked me for what I had done that night, especially that I had defended this policewoman; he did have some good points you see.

Another night there were three of us engaged with a real drunk. He was a fighter; it took three of us to subdue him and when we came to cuff him we hadn't a pair of handcuffs between us. He knocked all three of us down and was going to make a run for it, but somehow we got him and frog-marched him to the station about half a mile away, much to the jeers of the people around, not one of whom came to our assistance that night.

One Sunday afternoon in February, I was patrolling along the cliff top. There didn't appear to be much to do and I was, as it were, taking the air. Suddenly I heard a continuous tapping noise coming from the direction of an old wreck on the beach below the cliffs. Looking over the deg of the cliff I saw one of our local thieves disappearing through a hole in the deck of the wreck, which was three quarters on its side and had lain there for years; it was no danger to anyone, but no one seemed to want to buy the wreck even for scrap.

I waited, and before long up came the one who appreared to have been doing the tapping. I thought 'Aye aye, what's on here?' The other came into view now with a sack on his back, and then both began to ascend the cliff, just like a couple of smugglers. I waited, and when they got to the top of the cliff, puffed out with the weight they were carrying, they nearly fainted for they had both sacks full of copper scrap. They gave up right away, and I took both them and their loot to the station. The younger one got six months probation and the elder nine months inside. The case was tried at the Assizes, for larceny on a wreck can only be dealt with in that way.

The two brothers were a real nuisance; they had been caught before stealing cycles, and fined, and they were caught again and again for the same suspected offence, but they always claimed they had found the cycles and were taking them to the station. The two had a smaller brother who used to stand in the main street and tell all and sundry he was lost. He would get money and food and a great deal of sympathy off the trippers, till one of us came along. They were real devils, cockneys, evacuated to our town during the war.

During this period my wife and I began to get on well, we had another son, Christopher John, born in the local maternity hospital, and even that didn't go right for I had a terrible cold at the time and waited till two days after he was born to go and see him. Then they brought a baby to show me and I immediately said to the nurse, 'That's not mine'. She sort of looked at me slightly old fashioned and then at the name tag round his ankle, and it certainly wasn't Christopher but another baby, named Cooper. Then I saw Chris, he was a real chubby little chap and I was as pleased as a dog with two tails when I brought him home. With the sea air every day he grew into a great big strong lad. We kept him in the open air all the time except for feeding. I was proud to push his pram, but I was also afraid he might get leukaemia. However, he has grown into a fine man and is married with his own home and family.

Chapter 12. My Own Beat

Not long after Christopher was born I was transferred and given my own beat, an area of about fourteen square miles right out in the country. When transferring we had three days off, the day before, the day of the move and the day after to get settled in; the move usually took place on a Tuesday.

Well on the Thursday night of that week I went out on my first patrol. I had decided to do 6 p.m. till 2 a.m. thinking that with little about I could have a good scout round and get the lie of the land, find my beat limits and get to know just what I had to look after. Everything went well until I came to a pub called the Victoria at about 10.30 p.m. - there was no TV extension and licensing hours should have ended at 10 p.m. I could hardly believe my ears. They were singing in the pub, which consisted of one large room and cellar, and as I went in the main door, a couple went out at the back. As I entered there was dead silence. I asked who was the licensee. A woman came forward and I asked her if she had an extension of licence and was told that she had. So I asked her to produce the document to prove this, which would have come from the local Magistrates. She said 'Oh, I haven't got one of them, our local policeman has given us one'. I said 'Has he? Would you get me a bucket please'. The bucket was brought and I went round the room and dumped into it all the drinks from about thirty people. They took this in silence and then I said 'I am your local officer now and I cannot and will not give you an extension. Now get out.' There was a general rush to get out of the door and when everyone had left, I told the licensee off in no uncertain terms. It never took place again.

Now the turning out of the customers wasn't the last of the affair, for next morning I received a telephone call from the officer on the next beat to me and in another Division. He was also a Federation Representative, and a member of the Police Council. He asked if I had been the P.C. who had turned the people out of the pub. I told him I was, to which he replied 'You're in trouble', to which I answered 'Oh yes?' He then went on to tell me that in the pub that night there were three magistrates from his Division and that they were going to report me for my conduct. So I asked for their names and addresses and noted them down and then said 'I don't think that magistrates are above the law, are they?' He replied 'Of course not', so I then said 'Well go and tell them that they will all be reported for drinking after hours', and as soon as I had said this the phone was slammed down. I didn't hear another word about the matter. I had no more trouble with pubs on the beat and there were seven. The news had got around.

I hadn't been at the station two days when I was requested to call at one of the main farms of the area. I guess I was getting the once-over. I went, and had a real long chat about the beat in general. He had heard about the pub episode and laughed over it. I was asked if I intended to keep chickens, and I said that I would have to in order to clear the garden up, it was such a mess. After a drink I went home and then things began to take place.

First I saw my garden gate being opened and in came a great big chicken ark being pulled by a huge dray horse. I didn't know who had sent it, actually it turned out that another farmer, other than the one I had seen, had sent the ark as he had heard from his friend that I intended to keep chickens. After the ark came forty point-of-lay Black Leghorns, all crated up, from the first farmer. Then came two hundredweight sacks of corn for these chickens. I was set up.

The first thing I did was set out to deal with the gypsies I had at one end of my patch. I gave them all a good look over; I had a good excuse for I asked to see all their Animal Records (movement) Books. Later on this was to stand me in good stead.

I hadn't been on my new beat for more than a month when I was back on the old one. This was in 1953, the time of the great floods. There were several people drowned, mostly American servicemen, and from the national news it appeared that our seaside town had been devastated. This was not really so, but the pier, boating lake, swimming pool, amusement arcades and the promenade were all wrecked (without loss of life) and scores of beach huts were swept away, plus a club and two brick bungalows which stood right in the path of the waves. The Americans had hired some of the beach huts and were living in them, normally these huts would have been empty for the winter. Several local

**Mr Macmillan in 1953
(P.C.Troup in background)**

people were drowned and it was some three weeks before all the bodies were found, the last being a little baby.

During the search for the bodies I met Mr Macmillan, later to be Prime Minister. He asked me what part of the town was wrecked, and when I told him he seemed to lose interest and soon left the area.

With the beach huts being swept inland for about half a mile, we had hundreds of people visiting our area to see the devastation and a certain amount of looting went on so passes were issued to those who had property in the area. On one day, along came a man and a woman in a posh car. The man said 'I've come to see my beach hut', so I asked him for his pass and he hadn't got one, so I told him to go and get one from our station. He refused saying that 'this lady' wanted to see *her* hut. I said 'Hold on old chap, you stated that you wished to see *your* hut, now which is it?' He then said 'It's hers we want to see', so I told them to go and get a pass, and not tell porky pies. The man then said that he was a county councillor and paid my wages, and then I gave him a piece of my mind. In due course I was reported, but I was only doing my job. One of our officers at a nearby village had collected all the people from the front in the darkness; he got nothing for his pains, but everyone else, bar myself, got a commendation. That councillor had cooked my goose.

The Americans came from their base at that time and helped us all they could, and seeing that we were not only getting wet but that the cold was eating into us, we having only our greatcoats for protection, the American Officer in charge gave myself and another officer a huge parka each. They were fur-lined and covered our helmets and coats completely. The thing they did best, though, was make us immune to the cold and we were extremely grateful for we were doing about twelve hours per day in the cold. Well our Superintendant came along and ordered us to take these parkas off - not police uniform you know! I could have punched him on the nose - still it takes all sorts to make an army.

134

Flood damage 1953

The Super later ordered myself and another P.C. who had offended him, to dig the new Inspector's garden; it was virgin land and we did have a job. It couldn't happen nowadays, but we did it and forgot about it. Nonetheless I was very glad to return to my beat.

I made several captures while I was out in the wilds and one rescue. The first capture happened like this.

One day while I was speaking to a gamekeeper, I learned that he had heard that some gypsies were going to do a raid on a farm which was not on my beat but on that of the Federal Representative. I rang him up and told him, but he didn't seem interested. However, as the thieves would have to pass through my beat, I decided I would take a chance and see if I could grab them.

I got a patrol-car driver to come along for the fun. He stayed about half an hour with the car hidden about twenty yards from a green lane which I suspected that the thieves would come down, but then he got browned off with waiting and left. Blow me, within ten minutes along they came, a tractor pulling a real good load of corn, diesel oil and Kositos (flaked maize for cattle). I got out in the road, shone my torch on the driver, the load and the faces of the others on the trailer. The result was that the tractor was driven straight at me. I jumped out of the way, the tractor, trailer and load disappeared into the distance and I gave chase. I asked a passing motor cyclist for the loan of his motor cycle, and managed to find the vehicles but no thieves. I recovered the load and went to find the farm bailiff. He didn't believe me at first, claiming that all his tractors and trailers were in the sheds, so we went and looked. The one I had chased was there, but another one was missing, so I telephoned my Sergeant and upon his arrival went in search of the thieves. We arrested two at their homes and three more in another town that night. They all got time and I got commendations from both magistrates and Chief Constable.

The next little tickle I got was through our baker. I had been to his bakery to deal with a fatal accident there; the heat in the oven had been too great, with the result that the pipes inside had blown up, the oven door had blown open. His roundsman, who was seated beside the door which was head high to him, got the full force of the blast, the door hitting him full on the top of the head. He was dead when I arrived. I helped clear up and drew a sketch plan of the oven; it was not a good drawing at all, as though a fly had crawled over the paper. At the inquest the Coroner commended me for my drawing and evidence. I was dumbfounded till I saw the drawing. It certainly wasn't mine, our Sergeant had re-drawn it!

Within a few weeks of this incident, I got a memo from the Ministry of Agriculture, Fisheries and Food to the effect that this baker was selling too many cakes to the Americans at the base nearby; his sugar ration did not allow for the amount he sold. I was detailed to investigate.

Now, I thought, there's only one way he can get extra sugar and that's off someone with a good lorry who passes through the village. I had noticed a big lorry pass through every Tuesday, and when it passed the baker's the hooter was always sounded by the driver. I knew the time he passed; I also knew the time he came back. I knew he didn't stop at the bakery, but just outside the village was a road junction, with huge oaks overhanging a large grass area, and a lorry could be hidden there I was certain.

I waited as long as I could, then, about half an hour before I intended to take up my position, I asked the Section Sergeant to come to my beat because I wanted transport for some prisoners. He hummed and ha-ed but came, and took me to my little observation spot and waited, not long, just about ten minutes. Along came the lorry and behind it came the baker's van. I got the Sergeant to start up his vehicle, but it refused to start, so I ran and lo and behold, just where I thought the job would be done, were the baker and the driver of the lorry. I edged along and saw that the vehicles were back to back. I heard the driver say 'Five pounds the lot' and he unloaded ten brown packets about 18" x 18", each weighing a quarter of a hundredweight. The baker then put these into his vehicle and handed over the money. At this point I came out of the darkness and the saucy baker said to me 'Want a lift Jack?' I informed him that I didn't but that I was giving him a lift to our Section Office. I told the baker that I was arresting him for theft and the driver for larceny. As soon as I told them that they were under arrest the Sergeant arrived, better late than never - still he was a good sort.

After that the enquiries were to find out where the sugar came from. I did about forty miles on a pedal cycle on this enquiry and found the chap who had been fleeced by the driver. He was a grocer in a busy village shop and when the man delivered he called out how much he was delivering, only he took one packet out of five, putting the new delivery on top of the old stock. Everything looked all right. and the grocer didn't check how many packets were there in the first place, signing that he had had his full delivery. He was shocked when I told him who had done this little job and that it had been going on for months.

The upshot was that at Quarter Sessions the baker was fined one hundred pounds and costs, and the driver went to prison for six months. I got a Commendation, plus ten shillings as a reward from the Ministry.

On 2nd June 1953, Coronation Day, I had two terrible jobs to do. I remember it was wet and the rain came down in torrents where I was stationed. Although my beat was fairly long I still did the patrols on foot and on cycle. Usually I pushed my cycle and went merrily along; this day I didn't.

It all started off at about 4 a.m. when I received telephone instructions from the War Office to see a family and tell them that their son had been killed that day on a firing range in Iraq. I knew this family quite well; their son was in the R.A.F. and the week previous they had heard that he was coming home for good. They had bought him a brand new Ford Popular car which stood in their driveway.

I questioned the need for going to the home immediately at the hour of 4 a.m. to tell them that their son had been killed, but I was told that a telegram had been sent and that it was better for me to deliver the message personally before this arrived. Anyway, off I went to this house.

Upon knocking on the door, the father of the dead boy looked out of the window and said 'What's up Jack, want a cup of tea?' I said I did and I was told to go into the kitchen and put the kettle on. In the meantime the father came down. As soon as he saw me he knew something was wrong, and without beating about the bush I told him to sit down for I had some bad news. I then told him the message. He visibly collapsed, his head fell so that his chin rested on his chest, he wouldn't look up, he cried, it was terrible and just as he began to sob deeply his wife came down. I let him tell her the sad news. She took it really badly, as any mother would. I got the tea ready and gave them both a cup and sat for an hour or so with them. The mother said that she had dreamed that this was going to take place and I left them both with their arms round each other, a most unhappy scene.

Getting home I was just taking my mac off when I got another telephone message, this time from a country force on the outskirts of London. It was about a young policeman from the Met. and his girlfriend who was a nurse. The young lad had finished his 2 p.m. – 10 p.m. shift the previous day; his girlfriend was at work at Wokingham in Berkshire, and both were coming home. The young lad had gone to the hospital where his girlfriend worked and picked her up. They began the journey, travelling by motor cycle, but both had been killed near Cambridge. They had run into the back of a stationary lorry and had been killed instantly. I was asked to inform the parents of the dead girl as soon as possible. This I did and in this case it was just as terrible as the first message I had delivered. I got to the home at about 6.30 a.m.; the table was already laid, for the parents of the dead girl had expected them home at about midnight. It was to be the day that she announced her engagement to this young lad. There were about seven in this family, all came down at my knocking and when I told them the sad news it was the father who collapsed. I did what I could, but did not stop for any length of time.

It may have been Coronation Day for the rest of the country, but it must have been hell on earth for both these families. Life is very cruel at times.

Besides tragedy, I also had many laughs over my duties. One especially I remember vividly which concerned one of the escape exercises that the R.A.F. ran through my beat. I made some six captures that day, all thanks to the children of my villages; I got on well with them and always found time to pass the time of day with them.

These exercises were run by the R.A.F. The participants had to make for a certain point. If they got to the point, back they went to their respective aerodromes, but if caught they really got a hard time from their captors, the R.A.F. Police and their interrogation officers. All they carried on them was their number, rank and name on a piece of paper, twopence and some toilet paper - no food or water.

Well, knowing that this scheme was coming off, I enlisted the help of my village school children. I had three churches on my beat, which were good landmarks and sure to be used by escapees, or so I thought. I had guessed right.

From captures made I learned that these escapees were making for a lavender farm towards the coast. Two I caught myself near to the churches, three I got through the children telling me that they had seen an 'evader', the sixth I got myself, a Canadian Officer. I was walking along by a hedge to get to some high ground so that I could see if anyone was in the area, when lo and behold, as I looked over the hedge I saw this officer just ducking down; he must have either seen or heard me. I waited till he was on ground lower than the hedge and jumped on him. He fell flat, all the wind knocked out of him. I sat on him till he had recovered his breath and the first words he said to me were 'Aw shit!' He took it in good part. I handcuffed him, took him to the nearest telephone box and eventually he was taken away to the cells where he stayed until the exercise was over. I daren't give him anything to eat or drink, for he would have reported me. It was good fun, besides being an exercise.

My next case was again with the Americans. Quite close to the perimeter of the air base, one of my gamekeepers had found four pheasant skins wrapped in the Sunday Pictorial, and along with this was a washing label with only a number on it. I have never known English people to skin pheasants at any time, so naturally I deduced that an American was the offender. From the number on the washing label I found that the owner was a Captain in the U.S.A.F. and his flight, I learned later, was next to the perimeter fence.

I went to the air base and first saw the Provost Marshall, he didn't seem too pleased, for Americans then had just come under our laws, but he called in this Captain, a decent enough chap but he had broken our laws and I was there to deal with the matter. He denied all knowledge at first, but then I chatted to him about U.S. newspapers and the 'Funnies'. I asked him what he thought of our papers, on a Sunday in particular, and he informed me that he got the Sunday Pictorial for it showed all sorts of photos in it and also had good cartoons. I then progressed further and he told me all about pheasant-shooting in South Dakota where he came from; he said they skinned the birds prior to cooking. When he told me this I went to my cycle bag and produced both the Pictorial and the skins, and at this he admitted he was the culprit, admitted the lot and told me exactly where he had shot the birds. I took possession of the .22 rifle that he had used, not for poaching but for using it without being the holder of a firearms certificate, and reported him for poaching. He was fined fifty pounds for using without a permit and also fifty pounds for poaching. His wife had been with him on his little expeditions, but he had admitted everything so I didn't think it worth while to prosecute her, nor did I mention her in my report.

One of my villagers informed me that I should go and see what was taking place at a house rented by an American couple. I knew about this woman of the house; she was drunk nearly all day. It was nothing to do with me how she lived, but she also had two children and they did concern me.

I knew the woman was a drunk alright for she'd parade in the village with her dress tucked into her knickers, much to the delight of the old men and to the unbelief of the women; she even beheaded a cockerel in front of some of them (they did this in America, so I was told). Anyway, I got up to the house and close to the wall of the house was a wired up lean-to which normally would have done for chickens. Well, what I saw staggers me even now. There were her two small sons aged about six years in the lean-to, and they just cowered there. Each had a dog collar round his neck and was tied to a wall. I noted also that their little legs, from ankles to thighs, had large red welts on them, not one or two but about twenty to thirty. I immediately took care of the children and, using the phone of the house, I called the Provost Marshall from the base. Down he came, along with the C.O. and the padre. They just didn't believe it, but the woman admitted she was the culprit in this cruel act upon her own children. I then called a doctor who examined the mites and then I informed the woman that she would be reported for cruelty. Well the C.O. and the Provost Marshall had a fit, they wanted me to forget it, but I refused and in due course the case came to court. This she-devil was sent back to the States, along with her husband.

After this incident I had a further dash up to the base. I was having complaints from local farmers regarding dogs from the base chasing and worrying sheep. I saw the C.O. and he made an order that all dogs must be kept under control. Well, on the way home I caught a dog after sheep. It was from the base, and guess whose it was, yes! the C.O's. He immediately rescinded his order. I saw the Provost Marshall about this but I might as well have spat into the wind.

Being on an outside beat, during the summer months we were sometimes called up to do duty at the seaside. Well one night I was picked for night patrol, from 10 p.m. to about 12.30 a.m. All went well till I was all alone and coming into a darkened area of the town. It was very quiet, then suddenly I heard voices talking and I heard one say 'When he gets here, we'll kick his bollocks in and belt him one'. I recognised the voice and slipped over to the other side of the street, and came from the other way. Didn't I give those two brave lads a shock! One was determined and tried to land me a punch, I countered him and really drifted him a haymaker, that flattened him, the other kicked out with his foot, I cut his other foot away and slammed him, then handcuffing them I brought them to the station. They were charged with assault on the police, and fined ten pounds each; both had records about a page long.

Getting back to my beat I just jogged along, and helped out now and again with tractor-driving on the land for a farmer, earning more money on my rest day than I did all week as a policeman. It was a good life and I liked it, but my wife hated it; she wanted to be back in London, that was her dream. I am sorry to say I didn't oblige.

On this beat of mine a teleprinter weather station was being built by British workmen, but for the Americans. I was asked to visit each day; I had the order from H.Q. to keep an eye on it and I did. One morning when I got to this station, there were several Americans about and the next thing I knew was that a gun was jammed into my back by an American soldier asking who I was and what I was doing. To think it was happening to me in my own country where I was a policeman! I saw red, and demanded to be taken to the officer in charge who politely told me that the Americans had now taken over and that they would have their own guard. I didn't half let rip over the gun in my back and when I had been escorted to the gate I asked this clot with the gun to step out into the road. 'You're not in charge here' I said 'I am, so just step forward into the road and I'll wrap that bloody gun round your neck'. The sentry didn't bite so I went straight home and rang our Superintendant. Down he came, plus the C.O. of the base, to my house. There wasn't half a row, but in the end common sense prevailed and the C.O. apologised to me. The weather station could look after itself from now on as far as I was concerned.

While out in the country you get to know all manner of little things. For example, if you stand at the edge of a field the animals will come over to you, or if geese are cackling there's someone or something about. Well about 3 a.m. one morning, I was out on a right lonely road, I knew the isolated pub nearby kept geese, and suddenly they started up a real chorus, so I waited and along came a small car as silent as could be. It was certainly not being driven hard or fast. I stopped the vehicle, and saw that the driver was the manager of the U.S.A.F. canteen. He told me he was on his way home and that he had been working late. So he had, but for his own benefit. I told him I was going to search his vehicle under the Poaching and Preventing Act as I suspected him of poaching. I certainly didn't really suspect him of poaching, but thought he'd been up to no good and I was finding out, which I did.

In the rear of the car there was a big heap of something under a blanket, it was full of goodies, chocolate, beer, gin, all sorts, and on the floor of the vehicle between the rear seats and the back was a load of about a hundredweight of anthracite coal. I couldn't believe my eyes. There he was with a twenty-five pound a week job and me on about ten pounds and here he was thieving. He admitted it was all stolen from the base. He first lost his job and then got a hefty fine at our court.

The next one I dealt with was a local Postmaster, a nice enough chap to talk to but... one night I stopped him with a load of berried holly he had taken from the local churchyard. He was one of the churchwardens and he had given himself permission to take the holly. He was making wreaths with it and selling them. I had a suspicion of this and that was the reason I had stopped him. I noted also that he was driving his own car with an excise licence outdated by about six months. The upshot was that the other churchwardens agreed not to say he had stolen the holly, but the excise licence offence he could not get off. I went to serve the summons on him for two offences, using the vehicle without an excise licence and making a false declaration to get a Licence. He made me read the summons out and accepted the first of not having the licence, but refused the other summons. I explained it to him and asked him whether when he made out his application he had read the bottom of the application stating that during the last year, six months or three months, he had been using the vehicle. He said that he had, but had not crossed out anything and bluntly stated that he had not been using the vehicle at all. I reminded him that I had stopped him just before Christmas. He agreed then that I had, so I said 'Well?', 'Oh I see what you mean' he said, and accepted the summons. All correct and above board, but wait. I called for him as I was going to court, and asked his wife where he was. She didn't know, but said that he had gone off at about 6.30 a.m. carrying a haversack, a towel and his shaving kit. She didn't even know he was going to court. I thought 'I wonder what the silly old fool means by this'. At court I got to know!

The Postmaster's name was read out, and he got up and went toward the dock. He was told to wait for some reason, then again his name was called and he shouted out 'You've called my name before, what the bloody hell do you want to sing it out for again?' I was dumbstruck, and the magistrates sat there with their mouths open. Then the charges were read out, and he was asked if he had heard the charges and understood them. He shouted 'I've given you my bloody name, I know what I'm here for, get on with it'. He was then asked by the Clerk 'Are you pleading guilty?' to which came back the reply 'I'm not wet. No'. He was then told to sit down and the evidence was given. He defended himself and after retiring the magistrates fined him twenty pounds for the licence offence and he had to pay a year's duty, and then came the bombshell. 'You will go to prison for twenty days for the false declaration. You of all people should have known better.' At the sentence he said 'Come on then, let's go'. I suppose that was why he took his haversack and shaving kit, he was going to prison, but he lost his Post Office, plus his shop. I really think the magistrates gave him the term in prison because of his cheek.

The last job I did on this beat was very sad, it concerned two elderly people who had been married about fifty years. They lived like paupers, and I was a regular caller at their home, if it could be called that. They always had newspapers on the table for cloths, orange boxes for chairs, but the place was spotless; it always smelled of carbolic soap. Neither would go into a home, for they imagined they would be separated. They never had any lights on in their hovel, for that it most certainly was. They drew their pensions, ate their food and did nothing else. There were no carpets on the floor, just the table and two boxes. I used to feel sorry for them and dropped a pheasant in every now and again, but they would never let me into the house. The lady, she would have been about seventy-five years old and Charlie was about eighty. They just wouldn't accept charity and just existed.

One day at about 8 a.m. the local butcher came to my house and said 'The old girl's up the street, she's shouting out that Charlie is dead'. I didn't ask who he meant but went at once to the old couples' home. The woman let me in (this was the very first time) and I saw what I have described before. I asked her what she meant, 'Yes,' she said 'Charlie's dead'. I asked her to take me to him. Well, he was dead all right, he must have been dead about a week. I noted that there were two single beds in the room. The body was on one, stiff and stark, and as cold as ice, although it was summer. I asked when he had died, she replied 'This morning'. I asked how she knew this and she said 'He winked'. One eye was open and the other closed. It had opened, or shut as the case may be, as she had looked at him that morning. There was no inquest; he had died of a burst stomach through cancer. What a terrible lonely death. The old lady was taken into care, and that was the last I heard of her.

Now the next job I did was a few days after this death; every day brought a new experience. There were several big farms in the area, and the owner of the biggest, some two thousand acres or more, was a real gentleman. They had about twenty tractors always going at one time and they employed several men as you can imagine, and two full time mechanics. One of the mechanics had also set up in business on his own in a nearby town; he was doing very well, and was highly thought of both by this farmer and others, especially if these others owned John Deere tractors. He was a dab hand at repairing these.

Now before I got to this beat, several items had been stolen from this farm, and in particular from John Deere tractors which were used on the farm; starter motors, brake linings, brakes, lamps, anything that was moveable had been stolen, and no one had been caught. One day, through an informant, I learned that the head mechanic was offering John Deere spare parts at the local market at a greatly reduced rate, so calling a patrol car driver we went in civvies to see this mechanic and his stall. Sure enough, there were the spares all on view, I didn't say anything and rang John Deere at Welwyn Garden City. They certainly hadn't supplied the mechanic with any spare parts and greatly resented the fact that they were being sold so cheaply.

I made enquiries as to where the mechanic had his workshop, it was in a hall which actually was part of a pub. Good, I thought, no need for a warrant there. I saw the licensee and told her that I wanted to inspect all her premises, especially where the mechanic had his stall set out. She agreed that it was part of the licensed premises, so in I went with our driver. Well it was an Aladdin's cave; all the John Deere stuff, though, was hidden away. We found it and left it where it was; there were other makes also, but I couldn't prove where they had come from. Some were secondhand; the stuff I was after was brand new. I warned the licensee not to tell the mechanic about my visit and left the area, returning at about 7 p.m..

On entering where our jolly mechanic was working, he greeted us warmly, 'Always glad to help the Police'.... I told him the nature of my enquiry, and he said 'Go on, search, you'll find nothing here'. If he thought I came up on the last shower of rain I was going to enlighten him. Well we searched, and made a haul of about five hundred pounds worth of spares, all new. He confessed in the end that they had all been stolen, saying 'Well, he shouldn't have been so soft, it was easy'. There was so much stuff that we had to hire a lorry to take it to the Section Office, and later to court. He was only fined fifty pounds as the goods had been recovered, and he pulled out a cheque book and paid his fine by cheque. As he left the court he gave me the 'V' sign; I could have sloshed him. At least he lost his job and his reputation.

Now although I was on an outside beat I got quite a lot of duty with the patrol car. Many a night, when we were out, we had some fun as well.

On the long stretches of country road we would have the lights out and run as fast as we could and get some rabbits. Many of these we left at outlying stations besides taking two or three home for our own use. It was tragic when myxomatosis was about. I never will believe that rabbits did all the damage the farmers made out; they were the farmworkers' perks, and the farmers themselves helped spread the disease so as to rid the countryside of the rabbit population. Thousands of rabbits died this way; it was a crying shame, for at the time farmworkers were only paid about thirty-five shillings per week, a mere pittance considering what their employers were making. I like the men who work on farms, they are the salt of the earth.

Poachers were a pain in the neck, not the normal farm labourers, but those who came from another county with big cars and many guns, sometimes five at a time. We did our best to catch them, but it was nearly hopeless. However, if a gun went off near any of the Royal Estates, well it was worse than murder. Nearly every car in the locality was used to chase these vehicles, sometimes successfully, and all the gamekeepers came out; it was as though we were after Jack the Ripper. Pheasants are protected better than property.

I caught three poachers one Sunday afternoon, all on my own. They had a right shock and so did I. I was just pootling along and there they were, no trouble. They had come from another district and were dealt with there; they all pleaded guilty.

Now if anyone could get into trouble through no fault of their own, I could. I was on early turn, it was a bitter cold day and although there was a hut nearby, that wasn't for me, it was to keep the telephone warm. We were not allowed to use the hut, snow, rain, hail or shine. That telephone, how I blessed it! Anyway I was on main gate duty at a royal residence, and up came a really delapidated ex-R.A.F. vehicle. The driver was an elderly man, a gentleman by his speech. I stood there frozen, the ground was really wet underfoot and I had done about six hours of my shift when it happened. The elderly man got out of his vehicle; he was as smart as his vehicle which was a shambles, being dressed as he was in old khaki trousers and open-necked shirt, and if I remember correctly, he wore a soft hat with a feather.

146

Now there are numerous cranks wishing to see the royal family and my job was to sort these out. If anyone got into the grounds who had no real business there, it was a sure thing that they would end up with a three weeks spell in a mental hospital. Thinking of this I thought, well here goes another one, this blighter isn't passing me on any pretext.

The old chap informed me that he wanted to see the Queen Mother, 'What does she want to see you for? What's special about you?' I asked. He replied 'I'm a painter', and I said 'So what?' and the man said 'I'm Mr Seago' to which I said 'Who's he?. Go on, be off before you get yourself and me into trouble'. He still persisted, so I told him where the duty Sergeant was and directed him the way to go. That was the last I saw of him, but not the last I heard!

Well about half an hour later I saw the duty Sergeant; he was wild, I could see, and I thought the old man had given him a bit of trouble and he was coming to vent his spleen on me. He was coming to do the latter alright. He almost ran at me saying 'You've done it this time, you're for the high jump'. I asked what I had done, and I was told that I hadn't let this Mr Seago in. 'Well,' I said 'no one told me he was coming and I didn't know the man, so I sent him to you'. Well this took the wind out of the Sergeant's sails alright. No one *had* told me. I had done my duty and that was that. However I was enlightened as to who this Mr Seago was; he was a painter alright, a 'Painter of Wildfowl on The Wing', and the Queen Mother was his patron. Nothing happened to me and in later years the Sergeant and I became good friends. He was as straight as a die, a real good bloke.

The last winter I had on my 'beat on the prairie' as I called it, I seemed to live at court. The Chief Constable didn't like his men having a lot of court appearances; he thought that it was best to let things just glide along, tell people off and just keep a general eye on things.

But this winter we had a blizzard, a real snorter. I was cut off for a week; nothing got through, but despite the snow the telephone was never put out of order. It was all go, and the Americans proved their worth that winter in more ways than one.

The snow started at about 6 p.m. in the evening. Next day I went to court and got a lift home by car, leaving my cycle at the Section

Office. By nightfall the coastal roads were all blocked. That night there was a meeting for Special Constables which I had to attend, so I got a lift there and back. That was a fatal mistake, for next day I was snowed in. I rang the Section Office and asked about my cycle; I was told to come and get it. Now that presented a problem. I told the Sergeant the snow was about two feet deep outside my gate, but he said I had left the cycle, so I could come and get it. Well, off I went trudging through the snow, in places it was four feet deep, but after about four hours I got my cycle. It was seven miles home and I carried the cycle all the way with one stop at a lonely farm labourer's cottage where I thawed out and had a real good mug of hot sweet tea. From there I had another four miles to go; the snow froze on my face and when I got indoors it fell off in one sheet. I was so tired I just sat down and went off to sleep. At about 6 p.m. after I had had a meal the phone bell went. It was the Superintendant who informed me that I was to await the arrival of an American ambulance which was going to try and break through to a coastal village where a woman had fallen and smashed her kneecap and a motorist had been injured after running into a petrol tanker. I was to guide it, for except for tall trees you couldn't see the roads or fields. We were to take the injured people to the R.A.F. Station, then a U.S.A.F. base, and from there they would be transferred to another ambulance and taken to hospital.

In due course the ambulance arrived, it was fitted with a snorkel which meant if need be it could go under water. The driver was a great big black Sergeant, and there were two other attendants. From my house it was not too bad; we just pushed the snow in front of us. Then suddenly we hit a bad patch and the snow went right over the cab. The driver reversed and then we kept hitting the snow head-on till we broke through. I stood on the running board looking for landmarks, which were few and far between, but after about seven hours we got to the coast and picked the man up, wrapping him up in blankets and bear rugs. He was in a really bad way so I decided we wouldn't go for the woman straight away; she was in no danger and she was at home, whereas this man needed help badly.

The journey back was nearly as bad, but some of our tracks were still there so, although we still had to reverse now and again and hit the snow, we got through. What a ride! At times the snow was over the top of our vehicle, but we made it to the base. The man was examined by service doctors and X-rayed; his ribs were crushed, one femur was broken and he was unconscious. We had a meal, but the ambulance we expected did not arrive, so off we went again and arrived at about 10a.m. at the big hospital to be greeted with 'You took your time, didn't you'. Thirty hours we had been on the road! It was alright for them, for there was little or no snow in the main town - the coast had caught the lot.

Having delivered our patient we made our way back intending to go for the woman, but our radio eventually picked us up when we were nearly there and we were told that she had been taken by a normal ambulance as the main road had been partially cleared.

On the way back we found an elderly man in a Rolls-Bentley with his vehicle head-on into a deep snow-drift. It was lucky we saw him but the shiny roof of the vehicle gave it away so we stopped, and I went to investigate. I spoke to the old gentleman and said 'Who the hell are you? You must be mad being out in weather like this. What's your name?' He said he was the Earl of L. and 'Yes I am a bloody fool, can you help?'. Out popped the G.I's and shovelled the snow away, and as the vehicle wouldn't start we towed it to a farm nearby. When the farmer saw who we had with us he got his own car out of his barn and put the Rolls in; his own vehicle was left out in the open. We got the Earl home and he invited us in to dinner, but we declined. We were too dirty. He was so grateful that he gave us all permission to shoot over his land and use his guns whenever we wanted to. I don't know if the Americans took up the offer, but I did and had many a good day shooting on my own.

Back at my home about nine o'clock at night, I got a telephone call to get out and look for a certain Earl, who was missing, believed to be somewhere between my patch and Cambridge. I told the caller, a Superintendant of another Division to my own that this couldn't be so, for I had taken him home some hours ago. I was asked why I hadn't reported the matter, I just said that I hadn't because I wasn't asked. So ended that bit of excitement. It was in all the national papers; we all got a great write up and my report was printed verbatim in the local press.

I saw the Earl of L. several times after that at race meetings and at the church where the royal family worshipped. He always came over and spoke to me and on one occasion he told me that if ever I wanted any help in anything, he would give it to me.

I was just cycling along one night, about 7 p m , thinking how nice and quiet things were, when a jeep came roaring up and stopped. It was full of 'Snowballs' and when I enquired what they were after, they informed me that a black G.I. had attempted to rape a white girl, a woman on my beat. They all had their pistols out and were ready to shoot this black man if they could find him. Well I enlightened them on that matter and went to the home of this woman and questioned her. The black G.I. had come up and spoken to her, but she didn't understand what he was saying so had run off. He had in no way tried to touch her, nor had he spoken to her harshly; the woman was frightened, that was all, for it was dark. She had run off to the main gate of the base and informed the 'Snowball' on duty. I told the senior 'Snowball' that they could go back to their base; this was my beat and I would deal with the matter. I wasn't half wild to think of them roaming our countryside with guns, ready to shoot a human being just on suspicion. Talk about the Klu Klux Klan!

I eventually found the black G.I., in quite a state. He even thought I was armed, poor devil, but I showed him that I was not, and in fact didn't even have my truncheon with me. Apparently the G.I. had been at the base only a couple of days, and all he was doing was enquiring the way to our village where he was going to have a drink. He had heard that black men were accepted in our village pubs, not like those near the base where they weren't tolerated.. I took the man back to his base and to the Provost Marshall, told him what had taken place and asked him to keep an eye on those gung-ho warriors of his.

During this period my son Richard was born, he was a good sturdy baby and was born at home, but soon after this I was given orders to move. The beat was mainly quiet and peaceful, but one incident took place on Christmas Eve when I put in an appearance at the village dance, I wanted it cleared up prior to people going to church for Midnight Mass, because the village hall was close to the church. I had everything away by about 11.50 p. m. that night, but not before I had heard who had won the raffle for a huge cockerel. I heard the number that had won and the name called out, a visitor to the village. Thinking nothing of this I cleared off home to bed.

At about 2 p.m. on Boxing Day, just as I was sitting down to my mid-day meal, there was a knock on the door and this visitor was there asking who had won the raffle. I told him the number of the ticket and the name, and in fact this man was the winner. 'Well' said he, 'I've got the ticket, but no cockerel, the parish clerk says that *he* won'. I could hardly believe my ears. I knew the old chap and thought him rather decent, so I took the ticket and said I would enquire into the matter.

After my meal I went to the village hall, found the dustbin and got all the tickets out, and one was missing, the duplicate of the winner. I knew a P.C. who lived in the village but did not do duty on my beat, so I went to see him to get some information about this parish clerk. I got his history alright, and also learned that this man's family or relatives were always winning the raffles, but other than grumbling between themselves, no villager would make a complaint. I told Ted, the P.C. what I believed had taken place and asked him to come with me - good job he did.

Getting to the house where the clerk lived, I had Ted introduce me. They knew me alright, but Ted being a villager wanted to enjoy this little matter I had in hand and was making a real meal of it. The whole family was gathered round the dining room table ready to partake of a real feast; a big roasted bird was the centre-piece of their meal and when I told the clerk the nature of the enquiry he said 'Honestly Mr Troup, I didn't steal the cockerel' to which I replied 'No you just thieved it'. I then asked him if he had his ticket by which he could prove he had won the bird honestly. He produced his ticket. He must have thought I came up on the last shower of rain, for the ticket was the duplicate to the one held by the complainant. How did I know? Easy, it had two perforated edges and was also the missing number from what I had collected from the dustbin. I then produced the winning ticket, the original No.49, with only *one* perforated edge. He knew that the winner was a visitor and not at the draw, so thought that he would get away with it.

I took the ticket from the clerk and also the bird from the table and wrapped it up in newspaper. And then the fun began. The whole family wanted to stop me leaving, 'You rotten copper, you're taking our meal, it's Christmas you rotten sod!' With Ted I pushed my way out, pulling the clerk with me. When I told him he would be reported for theft, he nearly fainted. Back at the Section Office, the Sergeant refused to put the bird in his fridge, so it went bad. The clerk got a caution by letter. Still, that stopped any more winners from that quarter, and it was some months before the family ran another dance. Since that time, when I meet Ted, he always reminds me of this incident, shouting out, 'Where's the chicken, Jack?' Poor bird, nobody got it in the end.

During the period I was in the country, relations between my wife and I deteriorated rapidly. She was, as she said, a Londoner, and I suppose it got lonely for her. I couldn't afford a car, our wages did not run to that, but there were a lot of perks. Our larder was always full, we had a large garden and grew most things for the table, potatoes, carrots, lettuce etc., and there were fruit trees. With the chickens I kept and ducks and geese, we were able to send eggs to the packing station, and G.I's were always asking for ducks which I sold for two pounds each, dressed.

At no time did my wife make friends with any of the villagers. I was away most of each day, there was no television and the news on the radio didn't interest her. She had the children, but not being a country girl she didn't appreciate the countryside at all. We had rows galore so I used to stay away as long as I could from the house, just to keep the peace. It takes two to cause a row I suppose, but my job was my livelihood, our house was free, and the children were growing up in a healthy environment. What more could I ask? I hadn't come from the country but I grew to love it.

⊰⊱

Chapter 13. Into Town

❄

Eventually the day came when I had to move to another beat, right outside a small town of some twenty-five thousand inhabitants, and it was here that my life changed completely in many ways. I had a lot more work to do and eventually became mobile, the terror of the highway.

I was sorry to leave my rural beat, but thought that now I was to be near a town, things would get better for my wife. They didn't, because I was away more than before.

We moved again on a Tuesday, lock, stock and barrel. I even took six chickens with me, but my dog I gave to a farmer, for it would have been cruel to have him where I was to be stationed, along a main A-class road. He was a good dog and loved children.

The day after the move I had off, as usual, to get things squared up. The beat had been unoccupied for two years, for the officer had been sick all that time and hadn't even opened the Police Gazette or Police Reports. These are received daily, except Sundays, on every beat in the land. The house was a mess; he had vacated it some months earlier and gone to live in a council house on the beat.

Just as I was leaving the house on the day I was to begin my duty, the telephone went. I was wanted; there had been a theft at a local garage. On arrival I found that ten pounds had been taken from a supposedly secret place, behind a calendar in the kiosk on the forecourt. It was gone and had been missed only within the last half hour.

There was a witness at the scene, a woman who lived nearby, who informed me that she had seen a pedal cyclist go into the kiosk and take the money from behind the calendar. Now for some reason I just didn't believe this woman. I cycled down the road to a big junction there and found the crew of a patrol car doing a road check. They certainly hadn't seen a cyclist for over two hours, this was the way he would have come as pointed out by the woman. She had given me a really detailed description as well. Getting back to her, I gave her a thorough cross-examination, and eventually she began to cry. I then asked her where the money was. She led me to her bedroom, and there it was, tucked in her pillow. I didn't arrest her, but reported her for summons, and eventually I got her to court where she was fined some twenty pounds She was really well off and there was no need for her to steal, but her husband worked away, and I feel certain she had lifted this money just to gain attention to herself, she being so lonely. Soon after, her husband came home and she was never any more trouble during the thirteen or so years I was on that beat.

Being on a main A-class road, I expected to deal with accidents of all kinds. In fact this road had the highest accident rate in the county. I dealt with some fifty fatals and hundreds of accident injury jobs over the time I was there. I blamed speed, for there was no speed limit and the road had no standard width, varying from twenty feet in places to twenty-four in other. There were no footpaths and the bus stops were all in dangerous places.

Getting to know my new beat was some job. I had about four miles of main road with about twelve miles of minor roads, several farms, various engineering works, and a tiny gypsy encampment; it was a busy beat with not that much crime, but enough. What trouble there was was generally down to two or three families. For the first two or three weeks I just went round getting to know who was who, and sorting out the lambs from the goats.

There was a council estate, some forty or so houses, and according to my beat statistics one or two criminals there, just minor offenders, one brewery, a couple of retired colonels, and a retired Master of the Rolls. The beat really consisted of three villages with a population of two thousand or more, four pubs and two schools.

One family was a real pain in the neck. Their house was at the beginning of a row of eighteen houses with a factory in front which was not then occupied. I found that in the evening there was an influx of girls who all went to this house. Then along came innumerable G.I.s - I hadn't lost them, even here. So each night, for some four days or more, I took a wander down to this house, and there was no doubt that they were running a brothel. I informed my Section Officer, but, being an Inspector of the old school, he didn't feel inclined to support my theory, so I went to the local Council Offices and found out who the tenant was. It was the husband of the woman running the brothel; she had two sons touting for her who came along in taxis with the G.I.s. Apparently the husband had left her, but I found him and told him that the house in my village was still in his name, and that he was wanted to declare that he had vacated it. He did as he was asked and the next thing I knew was that the woman and her two sons had been evicted. So ended the brothel. There's more ways than one of killing a cat.

One morning at about 9.30 a.m. I saw three dubious characters entering a building site. They gave me a funny look, so I decided I would have a look at them *and* their vehicle. I kept an eye on the three men (they all turned out to have records) and when no one was looking I lifted the boot lid of their vehicle and its floor was covered in feathers. No wonder they looked at me. Now outside on the road was a builder's bus; the driver kept hanging about, so I wondered if he had anything to do with them. I spoke to him and after a while he got into the bus and was going to drive it away. I said 'Hold on a minute, I want a word with you'. At this he got out of the bus and I asked him if he had seen any of the men poaching or if they had sold any birds to him. He was most indignant at this, saying that he was a Special Constable and that I could search his bus if I liked, hoping of course that I would take his word. I got into the vehicle right away and walked right to the end of it and back, naturally finding nothing, but I had seen a sack of good proportions to the right side of his seat. I went as if to step out of the bus but, as I took the first step, I grabbed this sack and nearly fell over. It was very heavy; I tipped it up and out popped twenty pheasants! The man begged me not to report this, but I got him to court where he got a hefty fine. His mates I couldn't do anything about, they were on private property and undoubtedly had cleaned their vehicle out by the time I had finished with the driver.

Within a few weeks of my working this new beat, at 6 a.m. one morning, I was informed by a farmer that he'd had some thirty hundred-weights of potatoes, already bagged, stolen from his field. I wasn't pleased, for I had only the previous day warned him about thefts of such a nature and he hadn't taken any notice. I rang the Section Office at once and told the Inpsector the nature of the crime, when suddenly he said 'Hang on Jack', and about a quarter of an hour later he told me to go to the Section Office, stating 'I believe I've got your spuds'.

What had happened was that, as I rang, he stood in his bedroom and a local villain had had the misfortune to break down right outside his window. His lorry, was loaded with thirty bags of spuds! He arrested him at once but I had to cycle to the office, a distance of some seven miles. However, upon examination I found that the sacks were not the ones that the stolen potatoes had been in, so either these potatoes weren't mine or that the sacks had been changed. The thief insisted that we had made a false arrest.

Without a warrant I went to the home of the alleged thief, and at my approach a little lad shouted out 'Mum, there's a bloody copper here!' The woman came to the door of her house (right out in the wilds of the countryside) and asked me what I wanted. I told her I would like to have a look around, and she told me I could. I gave the outhouses a look over - nothing. Then decided to do the house as well. She agreed and as I walked in I felt a loose floorboard. I lifted this and there were my sacks, all thirty of them. The thief eventually got six months for this little escapade.

At this beat I was now on, I found that I had plenty of youngsters about the place, especially after they had finished school. There wasn't a thing for them to do in the village, so I began to make a few enquiries with the result that I got several people together and we decided to form a Youth Club.

I wrote to and also visited numerous firms in the area, both in the nearby town and the local villages. I collected some forty-five pounds, and bought a record player, darts board, a draughts set, and a football; a local firm made me a table-tennis table, and with the village hall free of charge, we were set up. We had about fifty children, from the ages of eight years to seventeen years, and they got on well together. While I was there I had quite a lot of help from the villagers and I can honestly say that not one of them since then has ever been brought to court We ran dances, and trips out, all for sixpence a week. As I was also the Company Sergeant Major for the town and area Army Cadets, I had my hands full for a long time and I enjoyed it very much. I went to camp with the cadets but after one day on the ranges I decided to pack the job in. I got on well with the lads and officers, we were all one happy family, but after a day teaching lads to fire at targets, I thought to myself, blow this, I'm teaching these lads to kill, and when we returned from the camp I resigned. I didn't feel I was letting the side down, but it just wasn't right, so I thought, and still do. I am not a pacifist, but I don't like the idea of teaching children to kill.

During my period on this beat the regulations regarding the speed of lorries was lifted from 20mph to 30mph and as a result the road was widened. This did reduce the number of accidents, but they had forgotten to put in footpaths and bus pull-ins. I went to the surveyor and we went over all the road and eventually we got the pull-ins and the paths, but it took months.

With traffic generally being speeded up, I was asked if I would like to do road patrol on a motor cycle. I jumped at the chance and it was the best day's work I ever did while on the Force.

On the Norton 500 - one of the first four patrol men

Chapter 14. Spaceman

⊰✲⊱

Besides doing general road patrol on my bike I was a real dogsbody, doing all manner of jobs and going all over the country on errands, sometimes to Bristol, then as far north as York. It was really grand with the wind whistling through my helmet, and passing everyone, not even having to worry about speed limits. I enjoyed every minute I sat on the bike.

One early morning I was pulling along the main trunk road of the area when I received a radio message to go to a shed close to some isolated houses. Information was never passed in full as we knew, but could not prove, that the press listened to Police Calls, so all I knew was that I was to go to this shed. Who had passed the message to the Police we never found out.

I got to the shed, opened the door, and got one of the worst shocks of my life. A man hung there by his neck; his feet were about four inches off the floor. He had not only hanged himself but shot himself as well, and half of his head and face were missing.

Beside the wall was what appeared to be an old-fashioned pistol, but I soon found that it was a twelve bore shot gun with its barrels sawn off so that both were only about two and a half inches long, and the butt shaved down so that it fitted into the hand like a pistol. I photographed the scene, closed the shed and sent for a doctor and a vehicle to take the body away. I then cut the man down and had him taken to the mortuary.

I made enquiries locally and found that the man was a Post Office engineer, that he had a little daughter, but no wife. He had sent the child on an errand to the village shop close by and then shot himself. I found the child and had her looked after by neighbours till her relatives came and took her away. At no time was she told what had happened to her father.

A note had been left by the man, it appeared that he thought he had cancer of the spine - it was actually a slipped disc - and that was why he had committed suicide.

Another time I was again on the same main road and was called to a bungalow where it appeared that a very old man was missing. He had been seen in the morning, but when a friend called to see him he couldn't be found and the lunch table, which was laid out, had not been touched. The friend, the gardener at a big house nearby, told me that the old chap had lost his wife some two or three weeks before. I looked all over the bungalow but could not find anyone or anything to show me where the man could be. I went to the local churchyard and the village church without result, and then I asked this gardener friend if there was a well about the place. He confirmed that there was, but it was in the greenhouse. The well was at floor level with no wall round it and it looked black and deep. The water gave no indication of anything untoward, but I took off my patrol jacket, rolled up my sleeves and put my arm down into the dark water. I found someone; I felt a shoe and an ankle and I knew I had found the old man. Getting the gardener to hold my feet I put both arms into the well and began to pull the body up, I got it as far as its waist, but, pull as I would, I couldn't get the body any further without help. The gardener then got hold of one leg and we pulled the body out of the well. It was a job, for tied round the neck was a cord tied to a fifty-six pound weight. The body was extremely cold and the man's glasses hadn't even fallen off. Even if he had thought again about what he was doing the old man could not have got himself out of the well; it was very narrow and he had almost stood on his head.

He had left no letter to say why he drowned himself, but we found thousands of pounds in the bungalow, every jam jar and small box was full of them. These I handed over to the Coroner at the ensuing inquest. I was asked why I hadn't called a doctor. I reported that it was plain to see the man was dead, there was no sign of injury to the body and I thought it best to send the deceased to hospital where he would be diagnosed as dead on arrival. The Coroner agreed.

Sometimes at night I would use my pedal cycle, the villagers had by now got used to the sound of me coming on my motor cycle, and it would be a change for me anyway. I used to meet regularly with the P.C. from the next beat at the local call box. One night we got a telephone message there to the effect that an old boy was missing. He lived in a wood and there was about three days milk outside his house; we were told to investigate. It was eerie going through the wood. We got to this dilapidated house and sure enough there stood three pints of milk.

The front door was just on its latch, so in I went. Nothing downstairs except that it was a mess, so up I went to what turned out to be the bedroom. There sat the old man in his pants and shirt, apparently putting on his socks. He had one foot up and a sock close to his left foot. I called out to him - not a sound. I went over and touched him, and he fell over then on to the bed. An 'augh' came from his lips, no more. I felt the old man; he was dead and had been for some time, for his body didn't straighten up at all. I got the officer with me to go for a doctor, who in turn arrived and pronounced death. The old chap had died of natural causes and there was no inquest.

There were so many deaths I had to attend, I cannot remember them all, but one gypsy I attended was a huge man who had died in his caravan. He lay flat on his back fully clothed in bed, but his face was purple and his tongue, which seemed endless, hung almost down to his chin. Having had him certified dead, I had to get him to a hospital for a post mortem and there the trouble began.

We got him on the stretcher all right, and opened the ambulance door, but he was so fat we couldn't even push him in. I thought 'here's a right how-do if ever there was one', then, looking round the encampment, I saw a great big tarpaulin. With the help of the other gypsies I rolled him in it, put him on the back of one of their lorries and wheeled him off to the mortuary. Not a nice way to go!

Patrolling the coast road one Sunday at about 12 noon I was pulling into my H.Q. when I saw two motor cyclists, apparently fast asleep. I didn't bother them and went into our office and hadn't been there two minutes before an old parishioner came in to complain about two persons asleep dressed in motor cycling kit. I said I would deal with the matter and went to the scene which right on the grass verge of the main road at a junction, on the right on a long sweeping left bend.

I bent down to shake one of the young men. It was a hot day but both were freezing cold, so I bent down and took the helmet off one to see his features properly and when I removed the helmet the back of his head fell out, it did give me a turn, but where was their motor cycle? I couldn't see it at all.

Nearby was a big concrete dustbin lying on its side. There were no tyre-marks or anything near this bin but there was a great big scrape about two feet from the top of it, the bin being about four feet tall. This seemed to show me that the bin had been knocked over. I went past it into the very high grass and small shrubs of the area, and there I found the motor cycle; it had completely disintegrated, the engine, wheels, the lot were spread over a great area, the machine must have hit the bin with a terrific force.

Radioing up that I had to have assistance, I had put the helmet back on one of the dead men, and it just looked I suppose to passing motorists, that I was speaking to them, there were hundreds of cars making for the coast and I thought if anyone saw what had taken place the road would soon be blocked.

The duty Sergeant of the area arrived and he was told by the Superintendant to get on with the job. I was really glad at the news and cleared off on patrol. On returning to Head Quarters, I found that the men had been identified. Apparently the young men had been out for a light drink some time before midnight the previous day, they lived further along the coast and were on their way home. They must have been travelling extremely fast and run out of road. The bin was about eighteen inches wide and this was all there was to hit; otherwise they would have landed in gorse and grass. *Speed* had done this and their subsequent autopsy showed they had had very little drink. I did feel sorry for their families, their world must have been shattered.

Later the same day I was instructed to act as observer in the patrol car, a Pathfinder. My driver was one of the best in the county and we fell in behind a red TR3 doing well over 60 mph in a restricted area. The car belted through, overtaking everything ahead of it, never mind the oncoming traffic. Keeping some fifty yards behind, we clocked him at 60 mph through one village, but when we got to oncoming traffic we gave this up, for he was driving dangerously if anyone was. We tried to overtake where the road was wider at a bus stop but he had us off the road and in amongst the bushes. I put my crash helmet on and after going up and down hill for some further two miles, we were able to overtake and stop this maniac. I pulled him out of the car. At first we thought it had been stolen, but it was his vehicle alright. I then asked him under caution what he thought he was doing and he said 'I'm a killer'. He was a real sarcastic type, but I sorted him out alright. It appeared that he was the son of a butcher, and that the car had been given him by his father for a birthday present. I asked him where the killer came in, and he said 'I kill bloody cattle, you fool'! Well, I fooled him, for eventually he was brought before the Quarter Sessions of those days and charged with dangerous driving.

He fought well in court, even bringing a log book which stated the car was white. The Counsel he had engaged to defend him played on this, but both my driver and I stuck to our guns, for once he found we were disagreeing in our evidence he would have torn us to bits. Anyway, we won. The lad, for he was only twenty-one years of age, was fined one hundred pounds and disqualified for a year. At least we got a real menace off the roads. He tried to get his licence back after six months, but it was held that it was such a bad case of dangerous driving that the full sentence had to stand.

One Sunday afternoon at the height of the summer season I was travelling on an empty road except for one car coming from the opposite direction. I had a brand new BSA Golden Flash 500cc under me, and a new Flash Harry helmet. Was I in for a shock! On the left side of me was an open space which was the car park to an area for picnicking, and there was a sign saying 'Teas'. I saw the car gradually approaching me, and when it was about forty yards away I saw the driver point to the sign. He turned at once, right into my path. Thank goodness I was doing only 40 mph. I swung to the left, my right leg grazed his front bumper and I made it to the grass verge. Having got on to the verge I began to pull up, down went my front wheel into a deep rut about eighteen inches wide, up went the back of the motor cycle, I flew into the grass and as I lay there I saw the motor cycle coming down. I rolled out of the way and it landed completely upside down beside me. I lay there for a minute or two to recover, found my helmet was split open and then got up. My motor cycle was hardly damaged, just the windshield broken. I got the machine upright and then went after his nibs. His explanation was that his wife wanted a cup of tea, he hadn't seen me and had turned, thinking the road was clear. The driver landed up in court and was given a hefty fine; the only thing that happened to me was that I was deaf for about a week - thank God for the helmet!

Besides road patrol I also had my villages to look after, and here I had a real beauty of a crime to deal with. This involved the stealing of petrol from vehicles kept in a yard. Lorry drivers were finding that they weren't doing the mileage they should on the amount of petrol they were seen to be using. The thief got greedy and it was found one day before a certain vehicle went out that its tank was only half full. I was called in.

Well it was either the drivers themselves, there being about thirty employed at this depot, or the manager, or the foreman, or the night watchman. The latter was my favourite. I had locks put on all the petrol tanks, but still petrol was going, so I asked the C.I.D. for a colouring agent which couldn't be seen when put into the main tank at the depot. I might as well have asked for the moon !

Well one morning I called in at this depot and there was a strong smell of petrol in the watchman's hut. It was a Sunday so he was on all day. So I told him I had just finished duty and was going home and then to the seaside. I rode up the road away from the depot and towards my home, then I let the engine peter out, hid my motor cycle, and went back to the depot, but climbed over the wall to enter it. There was the watchman, a five gallon drum beside him, a cut-off hosepipe in his mouth, just ready to suck up the petrol and into the can. I stealthily crept up behind him and said 'How does it taste, old boy?' He nearly fainted. I told him he was under arrest for the theft of petrol and that further enquiries would be made and that I would get a warrant to search his premises.

I called for the C.I.D. to come, and away we went to his house. There were some five gallon drums of petrol around his house - about forty of them! He admitted the lot. At court the watchman was fined fifty pounds; he was lucky.

On another occasion a young lad on the patch, about eighteen years of age and living with his parents, told them that his friend had stolen twenty pounds off him. That was the allegation, and his parents had believed him. Both lads had been to a fair some twenty miles or so away from our village. They had enjoyed themselves there, caused no trouble, and got home safely. All well and good, but next day after this night out, along came the parents with the allegation against the other lad. I

163

asked the parents to be present while I was told this tale of theft.

Apparently the friend had ridden pillion both there and back from the fair. The allegation was that this lad riding pillion had put his hand inside the leather jacket of the rider, taken out his wallet, removed the money and replaced the wallet. It was not till next morning that the money was found to be missing.

I listened to this tale in disbelief. I asked if he, the loser, had ridden with his leather jacket done up, 'Yes' was the prompt reply. At this I asked the parents if they really thought I was going to believe this, I hadn't come up on a Christmas tree. I got right down to it then and after further hard questioning the lad admitted he had spent the money at the fair. It seems that the twenty pounds was his Hire Purchase payment which was due that day for his motor cycle. The father apologised for calling me, and I gave the lad the dressing down he deserved. I didn't see the other lad then. His mother was widowed and was, having a hard time to keep body and soul together. I saw the boy later and told him of the allegation and asked him to keep away from his lying 'friend'. He did.

One of the most tragic accidents I dealt with was with a young man who must have had a great sense of honour, but not of responsibility. He was under twenty years of age and deliberately killed himself. He had put his intentions down on paper in the form of a letter to the Police which we found on his body.

He had been going out with some girl or other, we never did find out who, nor did his parents know about the matter either. She may have been married for all we knew. Anyway, riding his motor cycle, he drove along the main trunk road through my patch, and on a bend to the left where a churchyard wall was the boundary, he carried on full pelt. He must have been doing about one hundred miles per hour. Instead of taking the bend to the left he carried on, straight into a letter box fitted into the churchyard wall, right through the box and into the churchyard. He didn't have a hope. Nowadays putting a girl in the family way doesn't seem to mean a thing, but this was why he had killed himself, poor lad. I did feel sorry for him.

◆❉◆

164

One weekend I was ordered by our Assistant Chief Constable to go to a certain road and to find out why we were having traffic jams of about five to six miles long. This was in my patrol area, but at weekends this was left to the town police to deal with. I kept on the other side of the town. I was not under any circumstances to tell the Superintendant of that Division, but to report direct via memo to H.Q. and the Assistant Chief Constable in particular, for he suspected that there were too many men doing overtime over these traffic jams. You see we did not get paid overtime, but got time off in lieu.

I went to the area and the traffic was really blocked. Stuck right in the middle of it with a Sergeant in a patrol car who apparently thought it a huge joke. Anyway, the traffic was at a standstill; I pulled up once and three cars collided behind me. I reported the drivers for 'driving without due care'; they were watching me and not the road. When I got into the town it was plain to see what was taking place. There was this big roundabout and I counted nine P.Cs. all waving their arms about and really making a real mess of the flow of traffic. This was the bottleneck, there was no doubt. I took all their names and in due course reported the matter.

Well, on the following Tuesday I was called to the town's H.Q.; the Superintendant wanted to see me. He called me all the names under the sun for reporting about the number of men doing traffic duty and stated that I had ruined their overtime. Most of all he was furious that he had not been informed of what I was doing. He didn't like it one bit.

Anyway, the following week all the officers had been removed from the roundabout, traffic flowed freely and except for a very minor stoppage now and again, we had no trouble.

One of the many laughs I had while on road patrol was an accident which could have been fatal. A timber drag is a lorry which transports trees which have been cut down and trimmed so that the timber carried looks like long extremely thick poles; there is no floor to this type of vehicle, only a long girder-type box with the brake and lighting control in it. The timber rides over this and is held in place by large steel posts about four inches square and five feet or more long.

Anyway, a drag of this type was travelling forward; it was signed up at the back correctly, the plate was still there after the accident, the rear light was also on and in position. Just as I was passing in the opposite direction, a Ford Anglia came up fast. He was going to overtake, but seeing me he braked, but not early enough. His car went forward and one of the long trees protruding to the rear about eight feet went straight through the windshield and out the rear window and there the car hung, roaring away with the rear wheels revolving like billyo. I pulled up and went back to the scene and stopped the drag for the driver didn't realise what had happened. The occupants didn't have a scratch. We couldn't help but laugh later, but I took the smile off the face of the driver of the car when I reported him for driving without due care and attention.

One night, over a fatal accident I attended, I fell foul of the Superintendant of the town at the end of my beat. It took place like this. A huge ten-wheeler lorry was travelling quite correctly along the main road towards London. Suddenly he had felt a terrific bang to his rear and his vehicle went out of control. He had not been travelling at any great speed and was able to stop almost at once. He found a big Rover car right underneath his vehicle; it had broken the axle of the lorry in its dash. There was only one person in the car and I could see he was dead. I called the necessary services, that is an ambulance, and heavy lifting gear, and in the meanwhile I broke the rear window and got in the car and managed to pull the driver out. He was an old man of seventy years or more, but there was a very strong smell of perfume in the car and it didn't come from the driver. By radio I found out that the old man who owned the car was supposed to have been, out shooting for the day. I looked in the boot and there were three or more guns and numerous cartridges, but the guns hadn't been fired. I circulated a message regarding the vehicle and driver asking if anyone had seen it prior to the accident, and also to find if a woman had been in the vehicle when seen. About an hour later at my house, I received a telephone message from this Superintendant, stating who the lady passenger had been, but saying that this fact should not be reported.

I informed my caller that now the lady was known it was my duty to report all the facts prior to the accident. The old boy had been having a day out with a friend in London, and he hadn't wanted his wife or family to know. On hearing I was going to put the name of the woman in the car in my report, the Superintendant slammed the phone down. I saw him later and he agreed that I had acted correctly in not missing anything in my report. Years later, when I was transferred to his Division, he always brought this up, telling recruits that I was a very good police officer.

At the post mortem it was found that the old boy had died prior to the accident. He was a lay preacher - no wonder the fact that he had been out with a lady friend was not for public knowledge. It was not reported in the press either.

⟩⟨⟨

I did duty several times as escort to the royal family and also duty at their home. This particular day, though, I was on road patrol. After coming through the wooded area from the house, having had to call there to see the Sergeant on duty, I swung past the main gate and on the grass verge stood Prince Andrew. I stopped, for about one hundred yards ahead I saw Her Majesty, on a horse. Little Viscount Linley was also mounted, and a young girl who later married one of our P.Cs. was the other member of the party. Prince Andrew asked if he could ride my motor cycle, I told him that he could not. What would his mother say, and wasn't that her on the horse coming along? He confirmed that it was.

Now in our force we didn't salute like in the army, more like a Naval salute. I got off my motor cycle and put it on its stand. I was forbidden to ride the machine when royalty was near, especially on horseback, and I thought to myself 'I'd better not swing her a smart and quick salute, it may make the horses shy', so as the party came close to me I drew my arm up nice and slow. Well, what took place would have had me executed in years gone by. The horses shied, right up on to their back legs, down came the Queen, and into the mud went the little Viscount. I thought 'Bloody hell, I'm for the high jump now, why does it have to happen to me?' It had happened, however, so I had better make the best of it.

I picked up the little boy and scraped some of the mud off him. The horses stood still till suddenly my radio blared out, calling me. The ruddy horses took off, the lot, all three of them, for the girl had by now got down and was helping me with the little lad. The horses didn't keep together; one raced into the grounds of the house past the P.C. on duty, the other two went in different directions, one to the left, the other to the right. Where they went I don't know for at this point I said to the Queen, 'Shall I go and find the horses?' To which she replied 'No! You spaceman!' Well, at that the whole lot of them walked off towards the main gate of the house. I went to my Divisional Head Quarters and there some more fun began.

I had to write all about the affair in the Occurrence Book, time, date, etc. I began writing and one of the officers came to see what I was putting down and called the others to see. Everyone laughed, and I can laugh now, but then it was dead serious. I thought I might get the chop. In the midst of this laughter in came the Superintendant. He read the book and began to laugh as well, for a while, then suddenly he seemed to turn green. 'Get up to the house', he thundered, 'see if that little lad is injured. If he is, you're for the high jump'. I went and enquired and one of the Metropolitan Police indoor bodyguard said that the child was O.K. and to forget it. Thank goodness. I told the Superintendant, but he didn't say a word so I carried on. I didn't let any newspaper reporter know about the matter, ever. It was just another of the troubles I could drop into through no fault of my own.

At this time I was still having not much of a home life. The Superintendant knew this, as did the Chief Constable, so that one day I came into H.Q. and the Super went for me and I him. The result was, I was told to report 'sick', and I was sent to the Police Convalescent Home, at Hove, Sussex; I had been allocated some six weeks stay and I enjoyed every minute of it. We were on the beach every day; it was a glorious summer and I had all of June and half of July. In the end I had to ask to come back.

The first day back I got my motor cycle out. I'd had the battery recharged by the local garage while I was away and getting myself into the saddle I blasted off; I did 110 mph just to blow the cobwebs out. It was grand to get the machine on the road again.

Back again on the road I soon had my hands full. I got a call from the officer on the neighbouring beat over the phone. Would I come out and give him a hand by going to a certain crossroads and waiting for a van which was believed to be involved in poaching. I went on my motor cycle and stood from 4.30 a.m. till 9 a.m.; it was cold, the roads were covered in snow and I was just getting really fed up with the wait when along came this officer asking if I had seen anything. I said that I hadn't even seen a bird, never mind a van, but he told me that they had to come my way, for he had found some empty cartridges which bore the name Eley on them and he thought that the men and the van would make for the City of Ely in the fens. I told him he was a real clot, over and over again, the name he had seen was the maker's name. Hadn't he heard of Eley Anti-Kynock cartridges? And he was a country boy at that.

In the area we had had a new by-pass built, and accidents on it were as frequent as hours pass in the day. My very first Inspector was the victim of one particular incident. His car had been hit by some driver who had just driven off. I was detailed to stop and deal with the alleged offender. I found him on the road O.K. and the damage to his vehicle was consistent with that reported, and the colour of the paint from the other vehicle involved was plain to see. It was dark when I stopped his vehicle, so I escorted the car and driver to a nearby A.A. Box and got down to the business of dealing with the man, the only occupant of the car. He gave his name as Hiram ...... His other name made me laugh. I thought he was trying it on, for it would have made a real Music Hall joke. He didn't like me laughing one bit and when I examined his licence I found that what he had told me was correct. It took me a couple of hours to deal with the man, all over my laughing at his name. I've never laughed at anyone's name since.

Chapter 15. Jack of All Trades

❉

By now both my sons, Christopher and Richard, had progressed so well at school that they both had places at the local grammar school. They were getting on well, but I was finding it a financial strain so I applied to the Chief Constable for a grant from the Police Fund to help me; this was a fund which had been accumulated since the General Strike of 1926. All Police Forces had benefitted and it was there to help police officers. I might as well have asked for the moon; I didn't get any help, so I got myself elected on to the Constables' Board of the Federation.

Each year at the annual meeting various cases of need were brought up. One was an officer who stated that his mother was on hard times. He told a real tale of woe, but somehow I didn't believe him, and asked for further enquiries to be made. His mother, it turned out, was better off, although widowed, than most of us on the Board, she had ten caravans at a local seaside resort from which she was getting the rent.

I had been given an enquiry regarding another old lady of about seventy-five years. She *did* want support; her pension wasn't enough and although she had Supplementary Benefit, she could do with a little more. The local officer of another force had visited her and he suggested that a grant be made, either in kind or money.

Well, with a Sergeant from their Board, I went to see this old lady. She had a lovely well-kept home and we had a nice chat and a cup of tea; we enquired about her monies, if any, and about what she had in the bank. I agreed that she needed a grant, but the Sergeant couldn't see that she needed a grant because she had a magazine on her table, an old one but nice and clean, and he said if she could afford that she didn't need any help. She could have got the magazine anywhere, she had not necessarily bought it. In the end I prevailed and we paid her electricity bill and bought her some coal. The trouble with some of these funds is that they don't like spending, and give themselves a pat on the back because of the accumulation of money.

I stayed a Federation Representative for two years. I did the job, but there were so many men who literally lied to me about what was happening to them that I resigned. I had lasted the two years and during that time I had seen the introduction of the Panda Car and Cadets. Both have their good points, but they have their bad ones too. Policemen in cars have lost contact with people. By not getting out of the car to speak to people and having very little foot-patrol the policeman has been away from his fellow man. A lot of criminal activity could be stopped before it begins if only the policeman would stretch his legs nowadays. Even on the motor cycle I had ports of call, a cup of tea here, a chat there - it works wonders.

One day on patrol I called at a village Post Office. I chatted a while and then the Postmaster said 'There's some funny people moved in up there', and he indicated a part of the village where there were several prefabricated houses. I nosed about a bit and found that three men, a woman and an infant were renting one of these buildings and that they were Londoners. They did look rough.

In our local Crime Information it was reported that a Hacker Radio had been stolen where a safe had been blown, so I decided to make a call on these Londoners on the pretext of asking for a gun licence which I said belonged to a Mr Ramsbottom, a fictitious name. This got me into the dwelling and I sat down and enquired from the woman, who was alone with her baby, if she knew of this man. She didn't of course, but on the table was a Hacker radio, just like one described in our local Crime Information as having been stolen at a recent safe-breaking. I didn't say anything but rang up our local C.I.D. and asked for assistance. I knocked on the door first. The woman knew me now, so she just let me in, and then along came the other officers. This was the stolen radio alright, the numbers matched, so we made a search of the whole place. I pulled a load of dirty nappies out of a cupboard and bundles of notes of all denominations fell out from behind. We had got our safe breakers and waltzed them off to the station. They were wanted by another Force for other graver charges. It had all come from finding the time to chat with a local.

What I object to over the Cadets is the fact that they come straight from Grammar School. It is their first job and they don't know how the other half lives. They are taught that this is an offence and that is, but they don't understand that a caution now and again helps with public relations. However, not all Cadets are like this; many have made very good senior officers, and good luck to them.

Complaints against the police now are dealt with by a very

senior officer. In our Force the officer dealt with things very severely; there was no hiding things up and the proceedings were fair. Somehow nowadays it has got about that the Police cannot deal with their own properly. They can and always could.

With the Federation out of the way I could spend more time on the road. I was my own boss, for I was governed from H.Q; they knew where I was, and all our officers had to do was phone up and the call would be put out to me.

One night I was on a road check, I had my motor cycle and we also had a patrol car at the scene. Out of the town came a car at speed; it didn't stop at our signal and went through the check like greased lightning. I piled into the patrol car and we chased it, got ahead and stopped the vehicle. I was sure that there was only the driver in the car, but an American serviceman got out of the vehicle on the left side. He said that he was only a passenger and that the driver had run off into some woods nearby. He must have been quick, for neither I nor the driver of our vehicle saw anyone at all, but he persisted in this story, so we called our H.Q. and an old-time Inspector came out. We told him the story (we'd already got the G.I. handcuffed) and our Inspector said to me 'Did you feel the passenger seat when told about this missing driver?' I admitted that I hadn't, 'Well you'd better let him go' we were told, 'next time you'll know better'. Of course the seat would have been warm, we never thought of that. There was experience talking when the Inspector told us to let the man go. The car *was* stolen but the story was that the G.I. had accepted a lift. I still think that that G.I. was the one who stole the vehicle, but we got an undamaged stolen car back, and I never forgot what the Inspector had told me.

In our area we had visiting us on numerous occasions a real villain of a gypsy who had more convictions than I have had hot dinners. I was sent after him one early morning; the patrol cars had missed him so I was sent to see if I could flush him out from some woods. The slightest sign of a police officer and he was gone. I knew he was in the area, but where? I had heard he was dealing in moss which he was taking from various duck hides, it brings a pretty penny sold to nurseries. So I hid my motor cycle under some old tree branches and grass, and I hadn't been hidden up half an hour when along came his nibs. I let him carry on, for I knew he had to return the way I was waiting for him. He went on and completely destroyed a hide, absolutely stripping it of moss. When he came back to where I was hiding, I stopped him. Without running over me he couldn't get his vehicle past me. His wife was with him, and I should have arrested them both, but he agreed to tell me of all the places he had stripped as long as I didn't arrest his wife. At court he got a hefty fine, but put his hand in his pocket and pulled out the biggest roll of notes I have ever seen. He peeled fivers off like bits of paper, and they say crime doesn't pay!

One day I was called to the home of an old gamekeeper. Some years before he had been badly beaten about the head by a poacher and the poor man had been left mentally damaged. Now he had got a real bee in his bonnet and was going to shoot anyone who came near his home. He'd got a little area of the village in terror and wanted to vent his spleen on one particular farmer for no reason at all. Anyway I was sent for, and as I arrived I saw the old man leaning on his gate with the gun at the ready, a twelve bore. I knew him, and he called out to me, so I just went up to him and talked for a second or two and he gave me the gun without any fuss. There were two cartridges up the barrels of the gun. I unloaded them, took the old man indoors and sent for a doctor, the local magistrate, and a Welfare Officer. After speaking to him the three of them decided that the best place for the old chap was a mental institution. I did feel sorry for him, but he went without a murmur. That wasn't quite the end of it, for his elderly wife took me to their bedroom and she showed me three kilner jars; they were full of strychnine. They had been quite lawfully held for use with sheep, but I showed them to the magistrate, and he told me to give them to the doctor. The doctor told me to dump them in the nearest stream! I told him not to be so soft and took them to a chemist for disposal.

One day I was en route back to my station from a Home Office check on my radio when I stopped at a café and sat near a lorry driver who had just pulled in. He didn't see I was a policeman, nor did he see my motor cycle. He went on something terrible about 'that cop on the motor cycle near the town where I live', - myself! I had to smile - he didn't half hate me. I left before he did and getting to my Police area I stopped him. He was taken aback, but after I had a long chat with him he laughed and said 'That'll teach me not to speak to strangers in a café in future'. I agreed with him for he had told me all about his load and how long he would be on the road. I could have been a thief for all he knew.

One Sunday I really got out of my usual routine of road patrol, at one village where there was a private airstrip a small plane had crashed, the pilot having misjudged the height of a hedge, there was no fire luckily, but he was badly injured. I got him off to hospital, leaving the plane well out of sight of curiosity-seekers, so that the powers that be could come and examine it. It was really out of my line of duty, so I went off to patrol on the roads, but I hadn't got very far when I received another call to go to my home area where it had been reported that a light plane had crashed on our common and was on fire. My wife had phoned the details in, all in good faith, but in fact there hadn't been a crash. What had happened was that the common had caught fire and a glider had been forced down and had flown through the fire. My wife, seeing the glider in the flames, had immediately rung for all the services to attend. I found the pilot quite safe, with the glider embedded in a ploughed field well away from the fire. Meanwhile five fire tenders arrived at the common, plus two ambulances and half the police of the county. As far as I was concerned my wife had acted promptly, it was just good luck that there had not been a crash. Still, the authorities didn't look at it that way.

One day I had to go to a large factory on my patch on enquiries. In their stores I noticed that they had all black-heat heaters, for there was quite a bit of paint about. But I also noticed a single-bar electric fire near a pillar and quite close to where they put their invoices. I didn't pay much attention to this at the time, but about a week later I was called to a great big blaze at this same store. It was gutted. Machine tools and all manner of spares were lost and all the paint tins looked as if they had exploded. I wasn't at all satisfied with the explanation given me by the manager of how he thought the fire had started. He denied that there had been an open single-bar electric fire in the stores.

I sent for the Forensic Science Laboratory Technicians from Nottingham to come. I explained about the fire and my suspicions, pointing out the area in which I had seen this open electric fire. With the whole place being gutted it was not visible at once, but on instructions from the scientists I dug down into the rubble and there it was. The cause of the fire, they deduced, had been this electric fire left on at night. A piece of string holding some of the invoices had fallen on to the fire and, acting like a wick, it had smouldered for some time till it had reached the invoices. and with the little draught there was in the building these had been set alight. No open-barred fire should have been in the store - their insurance was void.

Being in a county force is far better than a city, for there is a greater variety of jobs to be done and one minute there is nothing doing and the next you're right in it. One afternoon I was following a Vandan Plas 1300; I suppose I was about two hundred yards behind when suddenly it stopped, right in the middle of a three-lane road. I ran up beside it on my motor cycle and tapped on the window asking what the devil did the driver mean by stopping where he had. Well I got no reply. The elderly man who had been driving was looking straight ahead, his eyes wide open; he gave no indication that he had even heard or seen me. It was the time before seat belts and as I opened the car door he fell towards me. I pushed him back into the vehicle - he was dead. The vehicle's engine was still running but the brake was set. Poor man, he knew something was happening and had put the brake on, this being his last action before he died. He must have been a really careful driver, and his last thoughts had undoubtedly been for others using the road.

Another afternoon I was passing through one of the villages on the main road, when I was called to a farm entrance. On digging up the gravel to a depth of about twelve inches the farm workers had come across part of a skeleton, I told them to leave it alone and sent for the 'brains department', telling them to bring shovels and a good camera. We uncovered a skeleton about eight feet six inches tall! It was very old and brittle, the major bones breaking at a touch. How it had remained intact was a mystery, for cows, carts and lorries had passed over it for years, maybe centuries. We never did find out whose the skeleton was; no records were available, but nearby was a crossroads and the theory was that the man was a convicted felon who had been hanged at the crossroads for his mis-deeds, as was the custom in olden days.

175

Another job like that of the 'giant' came my way in a really out of the way area. An old manor house was being demolished and I was sent for. It was another skeleton, this time under the front door step, and it looked like the bones of a very small child. I was left on my own to deal with this. The bones were again brittle, so I took samples of earth from both above and below the bones before I got them out. I also photographed them and took them myself to Nottingham for examination. They turned out to be the remains of a goat. Apparently it was the custom many years ago, when a new building was put up, for an animal to be slaughtered and its bones put under the front step for luck.

Another day I came across an accident on a very minor road. On one side was a council lorry from which men were laying kerbstones. In the middle of the road was a small Ford Anglia car and embedded in the Anglia was a great big American Studebaker; it had gone into the Anglia as far as the driver's seat. No one was injured. Neither driver blamed the other, nor did the workmen who had had to dive out of the way, for the following reason.

A dark green 1100 vehicle with only a driver and no passengers, had overtaken the parked lorry where, owing to the narrowness of the road, this vehicle should have waited. Not he! He drove straight on with the result that the Anglia had breaked hard and the 'landship' had run into its back. It was a right old mess. I did what was necessary and, having got the road cleared, I was just going to pack up and leave the scene when from behind me came an Austin 1100 coloured dark green. The driver brought his vehicle to a stop, got out and said to me 'I saw a real bit of bad driving here on the part of an American about a couple of hours ago; he demolished an Anglia car'. 'You saw it all?' I said. He replied 'Yes, I was coming the opposite way and overtook that lorry there', pointing out the council lorry as he spoke. I said 'You're just the chap I want to see'. I then cautioned him. and told him I was going to report him for 'driving without due care and attention'. Well he just about fainted. To tell the truth I had no evidence that it was he who had caused the accident except that he drove a dark green 1100 and had informed me that he had driven through and seen the accident. However, there was no doubt he was the guilty party from his statement. The poor devil lost his job as a commercial traveller, got a fifty pounds fine and his licence endorsed.

One day I had a most awful experience. I checked a young lad for riding his motor cycle side-saddle. He was a real trouble to his old mother, beat her when she would not give him money, and cheeked her all he could. She was a widow of about seventy years; he was adopted, and she wouldn't have me do anything about him, but I still kept my eye on him, the only lad on my patch, really, whom I went out purposely to watch whenever I was on patrol. Having caught him riding as he did, I gave him a good long telling off, hoping to keep him quiet for a few days.

That same night I was at a Police Dinner. I was called from it to go and identify a youth killed while riding a motor cycle. He had come round a dangerous bend on the coast road and had a head-on crash. His poor body was a mess; I found his left foot in a motor cycle boot he had been wearing, about twenty feet inside a field. I took no part in the investigation of the accident other than to see his poor mother and get a statement from her as to when he had left home. She really didn't deserve this though she had really spoilt the lad, giving in to him in everything. She didn't believe me at first, but when it dawned on her, she didn't last long after that; she passed away within six months. You could say that the accident was fatal to two people.

Another brute of a lad I dealt with, of about eighteen years of age, was also spoiled. His parents gave in to him over most things. I was passing the home one day when the lad's mother came out and asked me how her son could join the Police Service. 'Lord help us' I thought. The mother informed me that her son was going to join the Metropolitan Police and that he would join the C.I.D. I honestly think that she thought her lad would go straight into the C.I.D. and that the Police in general were just waiting for him. One day I called at the house on her request; the lad lay on the floor screaming at her. He wanted her to buy him something or other, and he kicked and shouted. I told him to shut up and get up. He didn't like that and I thought 'Some Police Officer you'll make, Sonny Jim'.

About a month later this lad was driving his car in the opposite direction to me, and he gave me a two fingered salute. I let him carry on and about five hours later drew up in front of him as he left work. He had several excise licences cut up to make one. From a distance it looked as if the licence was correct, but on examining it I found that it was made from three. I asked him if he had placed this on the vehicle,

177

he agreed that he had and I had great pleasure in reporting him. He was later fined a hundred pounds. His career in the C.I.D. ended that day.

It was about 1960 when it was decided to alter our Police House. From the outside police houses looked quite grand, and they were well built I must say, but that is all. We had no bathroom at all; the bath was just inside the back door, covered by a wooden flap. Each time the bath was used I hoped we would have no callers, for country people very seldom use front doors. You can bet that no matter what time it was, there was always a caller when I got into the bath. A yell sent them round to the front. Now we were to have a bathroom.

Our big bedroom was cut by a third, and this was made into a bathroom, and my uniform cupboard became the upstairs toilet. With the bath came a boiler - it never dawned upon anyone to put central heating into the house. Once we had the new bath, we found that it was used more often, especially by the children, and soon the garden got flooded, so I reported the matter to Force H.Q. I was told to look for a soakaway; there was one shown on the plans, the house having been built in 1934. There wasn't one, only an overflow to the septic tank. No end of County Architect's men came and examined the garden for this elusive soakaway, but it was never found. One was built in the end and at least I was better off than the man on the next patch to me - he had paraffin lamps still, and had to pump his water up each day for domestic use.

Back on patrol again one day in late autumn, I was on the new by-pass, a great three lane affair. I was stationary, seated on my motor cycle, watching the traffic go by. From behind me I heard a car being driven at speed, it must have been well over 90 mph. I was fifty yards from the roundabout and the vehicle passed me at speed, no brakes being applied. You can guess the result; the car hit the roundabout, literally flew over the top of it about twenty feet in the air and there was an enormous crash on the other side. I raced off to the scene expecting the vehicle to be in bits. The driver got out and fell over; his four wheels were gone, he just stepped on to the road. How he got out of the vehicle alive beats me; all the glass in the car he had driven was broken and the wheels were off, but otherwise the shell was all right. He was a very lucky man, a German chef. He had just passed his English driving test!

During my period on road patrol I had cause to visit many a beat where one or two officers were really hard pushed to keep things in order. The fact was that a lot of duties now defunct had to be done by beat officers on behalf of the County Council. For checking gun licences, they gave us ninepence a visit, and we didn't mind that for we were paid extra, but normal police duties were neglected at times so that criminals 'passing through' got away with many a crime which normally would have been detected. One of these crimes was offertory box breaking in churches. Tramps, roadsters etc., were mainly responsible for this type of theft, but there was also the person who would be after antique candlesticks and chalices. Even the Royal Church on the next estate was not immune to an intruder or two. So one day, having had several offertory boxes broken into in churches along the coast, I was asked by a coastal beat officer, P.C. George Dye, if I would give him a hand in keeping observation on a particular church, for the officer felt that it was going to be 'done' as the saying goes.

Well George (now deceased) and myself hid ourselves up this night. We had been near the church for some four hours and it was getting really boring for it was autumn and pretty cold, when suddenly a figure dressed in a long coat and wearing a cap came down the path to the church door. We couldn't actually make out who it was, but into the church went this man. We waited about five minutes and crept towards the church door. Suddenly the man came out and we collared him; I jumped on his back and George gave him a right belter in the stomach, Down went the man with a yell. I turned him over and nearly had a fit. Guess who it was - our own Inspector! He was livid. What he wasn't going to do to us was nobody's business for we were laughing like mad. He didn't think it was funny, I can tell you. When he calmed down, he really couldn't say anything, for we were doing this duty off our own bat. After about a twenty minutes lecture he let us go, but he never forgot us, ever. The Inspector really was at fault, he used to sneak about all our areas and took a delight in catching young officers out at some minor indiscretion or other.

Another event concerning another Inspector wasn't so funny. I was giving a hand on traffic duty at one of the seaside resorts one Sunday afternoon, for the local men had their hands full. Having given the No.1 Traffic Signal (hand straight up with palm foremost) a car shot past me at speed, oblivious of my signal. Luckily no other vehicle was involved, so I ran for my motor cycle and gave chase, caught up, noted the number and overtook and stopped the vehicle. I asked the driver, a male about fifty, why he hadn't stopped at my signal. The man said 'What signal? Don't you know I'm an Inspector?' I told him that I had given a correct signal and besides, Inspector or not, he should have stopped. I also told him he was not any Inspector I knew and could I have his full name and address. I saw that he came from Peterborough. Anyway I sent the usual HO/T/2 away for a copy of his documents, he having agreed to produce them at Peterborough. Back came the reply; he was in fact an Inspector - for the R.S.P.C.A.!

One bitterly cold night in January I had been out on my motor cycle arriving home at about 10 p.m. It was raining that ice cold rain that can only be found on the east coast.   Having booked off by radio I went indoors hoping for a quiet night. About 11 p.m. there was a thunderous knocking at my door, and two locals came in to complain that they had been involved in a minor accident and their car had run into a hedge causing little or no damage.

In our force, no matter how trivial these accidents were, we were expected to deal with them. Now in between the time I had signed off duty and when this minor affair was reported the weather had turned colder, with the result that the surface of the road was like a sheet of glass, so I went on my pedal cycle, the scene being no more than half a mile away. You can imagine my shock when I got to the scene. There wasn't one vehicle in the hedge but about six, and another ten or more piled up. A post office telephone pole was down, and an electric light pole; there were three people seriously injured, one with a broken leg from a motor cycle, and two more with broken collar bones, all because these two idiots had left their vehicle at an angle to the main road near a junction.

I told them I was holding them responsible for this whole series of accidents. What with the ambulance, the Post Office repair crews and the electricity repairmen I had my hands full. I got various drivers to go some quarter of a mile away from the scene and help to slow traffic down. I was dealing with people till about 4.30 a.m.

I had no sooner dealt with this series of accidents than along came another; this time it was a Police Sergeant's son. The lad had piled his dad's vehicle into a dyke through heavy braking. The joke was that the car was insured for owner only, and that certainly was not the lad. I was asked by the father, when he turned up in a patrol car, if I would overlook the incident. I said I most certainly would not, and told him he would be reported for permitting the offence. As you can imagine, that didn't go down too well and he left the scene swearing like anything about me. Well the way I looked at it was that he wouldn't give me a job if the matter was found out and I was sacked. In any case, being a Police Officer didn't make the father and son immune to the law.

With the heavy spate of accidents I had to deal with, I got rather fed up with road patrol and it came to a head one night as I was driving home. First a pheasant hit me on the head as it flew over the road and nearly toppled me off my machine, and then I nearly ran into the back of a vehicle which I didn't see because of the sleet that was coming down at the time. It was a miracle I didn't pile into the back of it, so when I got home I radioed up that I was finishing on the motor cycle and would someone collect it next day. I was forty-nine years of age at the time and I thought that my reflexes weren't all they should be.

Chapter 16. End of the Road

Some days later I was asked to hand the motor cycle over to a P.C. from the town in the next Division. I was instructed to tell him all about the machine, safe speeds etc. which I did. One peculiarity about the motor cycle was that when passing farm gates where the wind was likely to blow hard as if through a tunnel, it usually went towards the centre of the road owing to all the streamlining it had. I told the young P.C. this, but first trip out, straight over the hedge he went. He wasn't hurt but he had learnt his lesson.

I was told by the Chief Constable that I could pick an easy beat after my years on the road, but every one I picked was either closed down or about to be closed down, so in the end I volunteered to be posted to the town. My wife was pleased with this, but as things turned out it was the beginning of the end of my marriage. She just couldn't settle. My two sons were now at the local grammar school, so it was easier for them, for the house I was sent to was in easy reach for them. I was put on an overspill estate, but did duty on the beat in the town.

Being posted to the town was a real experience for me. Except for the period I was at the coast I had little knowledge of how the town beats were worked or how we would be supervised. Well I soon got to know, for I found myself on a Relief team of six men, boys really, with eight years service between them. The Sergeant in charge was an old friend of mine. The shifts were divided up into three, 6 a.m. – 2 p.m., 2 p.m. – 10 p.m. and 10 p.m. – 6 a.m. There were no Inspectors on night duty and the Superintendant packed in at 5 p.m. We saw little of him except on the early turn when he came into the main office prior to his going off to the 'Holy of Holies', as we called his office.

There were four Reliefs, A.B.C. and D. I was put into D. We did three weeks on each tour of duty so that there were only three Reliefs actually on duty during any twenty-four hours.

In the station we had the usual offices, uniform main office where all enquiries, complaints and telephone calls came, then there was C.I.D., Admin. Traffic, Photographic, and Traffic Wardens. We had six cells, plus a large room for juveniles. The radio, teleprinter and telephone switchboard were all in the front office, all worked by the uniform branch, and last of all near to the teleprinter was the Collator's Office. On the upper floor, was the Recreation Room, Canteen and dormitories for the single men who lived at the station. We also had a firearms cupboard on the ground floor. There was a beat van for each Relief, and three Patrol Cars. All typing pertaining to Crime Informations was done in the main office by the Night Relief, there was also a bank of burglar alarms near to the telephone switchboard. The Division was connected to H.Q. by radio, teleprinter and by direct telephone line. Each man had a radio; at that time they were great cumbersome things and very heavy, and half the time they just didn't work. They were charged in the main office so you can see that the officer, a P.C., had his hands full when he was on duty in the main office. He usually had a recruit to help him, but at that time, other than a couple of typists, there were no civilian employees. All reports had to be typed by the officer concerned, again in the main office. In fact it was a real Fred Carno's outfit. No one seemed to bother about anything, usually the Reliefs gathered in the main office prior to going out into the street. There were Sergeants, Inspectors and P.C.s all in the main office as if they had all come for a meeting of the clans; it was utter chaos, and I vowed when I got duty there that I would try and alter things. Found Property was left lying about, Sergeants left their coats, helmets etc., in the main office and to an outsider waiting at the counter for attention we must have looked a real rabble.

On my first day I went along with the Duty Sergeant for a patrol in the beat van round all the streets and outlying areas. I needed this for I didn't have a clue where half the places were. I got some information from this ride, but it was not till next day that I learned a lot more. Being on foot is the only way to get to know an area. Seeing an officer on foot patrol these days is almost unknown. If you do see one I can guarantee that he is lost.

Luckily for me I was given almost a free hand as to where I patrolled. The town was divided into three areas, Central Beat No.1, surrounding the Central Beat was Beat 2, while Beat 3 consisted of the edges of 2 Beat. It looked alright in theory, but in practice it was hopeless. A Sergeant came round each hour to check where each individual officer was, and believe me he had a job as the patrolling officers were miles apart. We got a visit actually about once per night.

The Sergeant had his own work to do, checking reports, making out various duties and generally the station kept him in, especially if we had any prisoners.

The young lads were really good; it wasn't their fault that they didn't know what to do at times. They knew what was wrong, but as to actual practice, they just didn't have a clue. They were eager to learn and, considering the difficulties that they had, they did well. Some of my old Relief, nearly all in fact, are now senior officers in the force. They learnt the hard way.

⭐

Burglaries were rife in the town. It seemed as though the thief knew exactly what the P.C. on the beat was doing and where he would be. It took us months to find the culprit, all petty stuff. Offices where money was likely to be, and shops with radio equipment, were usually the targets. One night the thief made a mistake; he thought a large Chinese Restaurant was shut up for the night, he broke in and that was his lot. It was a lad on the Relief before ours. He was caught red-handed, and he got no sympathy from us, I can tell you. When he went to prison for six months we all agreed that he didn't get long enough. He deserved six years, for he had not only disgraced himself but also the Force in general.

Through my being posted to the town I was now living on a big housing estate, there were all manner of persons residing there, but everyone appeared to get on with their neighbours. There were Indians, Pakistanis, West Indians etc.; no one took any notice of their colour, but very few had jobs. Most people on the estate came from London on an 'overspill' scheme, so you can guess we got some right villains from that part of the country.

In the pubs we had the usual brawls, the usual arrests for punch-ups, but nothing very serious. Most times it was over girls who had transferred their affections to others; we took these as a matter of course. To be truthful, ours was a sleepy town and it was only when servicemen came into it that things livened up; it made a change and relieved the monotony.

During one period we had a spate of fires out in the country next to the town, no one was ever brought to book for these offences, for all were arson, there was no question of that, but suddenly the fires stopped.

One night I had been put in the office for a change and one of my duties had been to file the messages that had come in over a period, there were weeks of them, they were in order but not good enough for future reference. I got really stuck into this job and it suddenly came out who might have been responsible for these fires. Each and every one had been discovered by police and two names kept cropping up, it always turned out that these two officers had been on night patrol and one or other of them had either reported the fire or was at the scene. I collated all these messages together and sent them down to the C.I.D. and believe me the fires stopped. We didn't have any more for months.

Having been on the estate where I lived for about a year, I found that my next door neighbour, a West Indian, kept giving me some snide remarks about his not passing his driving test. I found out from his wife that he thought I had spoken to the driving examiners in the town and asked them not to pass him. Of course I hadn't and it took me ages to convince him that the Police as such had nothing to do with driving tests. His tiny daughter used to make me laugh. I'd come home always by the back garden, theirs was next to ours and if the little girl was there she always shouted 'Here comes the BUGGY MAN'. I couldn't really make out what she said, for my ear was not attuned to her manner of speaking. It took ages for me to realize that what she was saying was 'Here comes the Bogey Man', and having come from London it was obvious that she called me a Bogey Man because that is what policemen are called there. She was a jolly little girl. They left the district to go back to London, there being so few West Indians in this area. Besides, there was very little work in this area to suit them, and it is also very cold on the east coast and that did not appeal to them either.

One night I was instructed to 'pick up' a real character. He was no criminal, more an eccentric. I have forgotten his name so let us call him Bob. This man would have been about fifty years of age at the time, he was dressed like a tramp and mooched about the town at all hours. Night time would see him flitting from corner to corner; he would call in various bakeries in the town and then disappear, where to we never could find out. He was picked up annually, given a clean set of clothing, bathed, given some money and sent on his way. He never applied for National Assistance, and the tale was told that he was an old soldier who had been shell-shocked during the last war and that he was to be pitied and left alone. Not once was he ever brought in for stealing or interfering with anyone. He was just a character.

This night I got on Bob's tail, and I followed him all over the place. He led me a merry dance all over the town till we eventually came to a very dark alleyway. Down he went and I followed, but it was a dead end. He had disappeared and there wasn't a sign of him; he couldn't have climbed up anywhere for there was nowhere to climb. I tried several doors on both sides of the alley till I came to an old bookie's shop which had been empty for years. Suddenly the door to the premises gave, I nearly fell in and was confronted with a set of stairs. Half were missing, and it was pitch dark so I had to use my torch. I got to the top of the stairs and a huge black object like an enormous rat ran across my feet; I almost jumped out of my skin. There was a room at the top of the stairs. In I went and there was Bob, fast asleep. There was an old army coat on the wire frame of an old bedstead and an old sack for a pillow, nothing else in the room. I woke Bob up; he was really docile and he gave me a real old grin, and when I told him he was wanted for his 'annual' he came right away. One thing I did notice was that the walls of the room were honey-combed with holes about six inches in diameter. At the time I didn't bother to try to find out what those holes were. I got Bob to the station and he was taken to the hospital, given his overhaul, some money and sent on his way. He looked really smart.

On Bob's release I went with him to where I had found him. He was keen to get back there and I soon found out why. The place was alive with black rabbits - he had a real warren going there and this was how he had fed himself. Sadly I had to report the matter; the rabbits were destroyed and Bob must have found other accommodation. That night patrol was an experience I can tell you.

After a while our Sergeant was promoted from our Relief and became Patrol Inspector with the result that we saw very little of him. Our station was issued with small dictaphones which were to be used instead of us spending time at the station typing. It made life fairly hard for the Inspector, for despite the fact that the girls who did the typing were in the most part up to their job, many were the reports that had to be sent back, especially over charge headings in which a word missed would guarantee an appeal being made at some time in the future. We had a safe-breaker in and eventually he was given seven years. He had been caught en route to a job with the explosives in his vehicle. All went smoothly till after he was sentenced. He had been charged with 'carrying explosives' whereas in fact it should have read '*knowingly* carrying explosives'. That one word missed out set him free.

Most people think that because an officer is on a country Force, he is as thick as two short planks. Not so, there are some good men out on beats who are just as knowledgeable as those in the Met.

I was on Front Office Duty at the main station when a client called in. He had recently come to England from Rhodesia and he produced a temporary Firearms Certificate granted to him by the Met. It was for a Sterling Sub-machine gun! He was applying for a full certificate and really thought he would get one. I took possession of the weapon immediately. He even asked to be granted a dealer's certificate and what I learned from him took my breath away. He wanted to use two garages on the Council Estate as his store. These were very flimsy affairs. I pointed out this fact to him telling him that his application would be forwarded but that he had no likelihood of getting his application met. He went berserk. I also told him that there was no way he would get his weapon back. It was a Sterling Sub-machine gun forbidden under Part One of the Firearms Act and a prohibited weapon. He didn't understand this, so I sent for the Inspector on duty at the time. He had just transferred to us from the Essex Force and didn't understand what I meant, so we went and got the Act and read it up. In the end reason prevailed and the man did not get his gun back nor did he get any certificate of any sort, my report was fully supported by Headquarters.

Before long it was decided that our Relief wanted a Sergeant. I was called before the Chief Superintendant and told that my name had been put forward and I would hear in due course. I had been left in charge of the Relief for two months or more, so when I was again called to the Superintendant's Office I thought, as did the whole of the Relief, that I was to be promoted.

As I entered the office I saw four sets of chevrons on the table in front of the Super and all the other equipment that goes with the Sergeant's job. I was told to sit down and then given a letter from the Chief Constable. The sting came at the end of the letter; I was too old to be promoted and another P.C. on my Relief, was to be our Sergeant. To make matters worse I was told to take the chevrons to this lad, tell him he was promoted and that he was my new Sergeant. I didn't blame the lad, nor my Super, but it really browned me off.

For the rest of my time in the Police Service I more or less ran the Front Office, so I did not really have any more of the excitement of the chase and capture of criminals.

As to my private life, I was offered a council house in the village where I had been stationed in the past and I moved there together with my wife and family. Over the following few years my wife and I were not happy and for years I had told her that when the boys got old enough to look after themselves I would be leaving her. Well, things did not get better, in fact they began to get worse, so I did what I had threatened to do and left her. I had already met the lady who would be my second wife eventually, so together with her children we set up home together, with the blessing of the Chief Constable, I may add.

Some time after I left, Clarice became ill and eventually died and about six months later Valerie and I got married. Her children are all married with children of their own, but we also had a son of our own, Stephen.

A few months after Stephen was born (I had been in the Force for twenty-six years by then) the Chief Superintendant called me up to his office and told me he had been asked to recommend a Police Officer who was coming up to retirement age for a job as Security Officer for a local factory, and if I wanted it I should get down there and apply. I got the job and after retiring from the Police Force with a thirty year pension (my war service counted towards my pensionable service) I worked for this Company as Safety and Security Officer for ten years, eventually becoming an Old Age Pensioner at the age of sixty-seven, but not before we had another son whom we named David.

These two boys of ours are now in their early twenties and starting out on the pathway of life. Valerie and I live in one of the bungalows built as a Memorial to the Men of The Norfolk Regiment of the First and Second World Wars, so you may say that I have come, more or less, full circle.

Retirement day, 1974